Differentiated Instruction

A Guide for Elementary Teachers

Amy Benjamin

EYE ON EDUCATION
6 DEPOT WAY WEST, SUITE 106
LARCHMONT, NY 10538
(914) 833-0551
(914) 833-0761 fax
www.eyeoneducation.com

For information about permission to reproduce selections from this book, write: Eye On Education, Permissions Dept., Suite 106, 6 Depot Way West, Larchmont, NY 10538

Library of Congress Cataloging-in-Publication Data

Benjamin, Amy, 1951–
    Differentiated Instruction : a guide for elementary teachers / by Amy Benjamin
        p.   cm.
    ISBN 1-930556-55-1
    1. Individualized instruction. 2. Cognitive styles in children. 3. Mixed ability grouping in education. 4. Elementary school teaching. I. Title

LB1031 .B44 2003
372.139'43—dc21   2003040882

10 9 8 7 6 5

Editorial and production services provided by

299 E. Kelso Rd., Columbus, OH 43202
click@columbus.rr.com

Also available from Eye On Education

Differentiated Instruction:
A Guide for Middle and High School Teachers
Amy Benjamin

Reading, Writing, and Gender:
Instructional Strategies and Classroom Activities
That Work for Girls and Boys
Gail Goldberg and Barbara Roswell

Technology Tools for Young Learners
Leni von Blanckensee

Buddies:
Reading Writing and Math Lessons
Pia Hansen Powell

Mathematics the Write Way:
Activities for Every Elementary Classroom
Marilyn Neil

Better Instruction Through Assessment:
What Your Students Are Trying to Tell You
Leslie Wilson

Assessment Portfolios for Elementary Students
Milwaukee Public Schools

Open-Ended Questions in Elementary Mathematics:
Instruction and Assessment
Mary Kay Dyer and Chrsitine Moynihan

A Collection of Performance Tasks and Rubrics:
Primary School Mathematics
Charlotte Danielson and Pia Hansen

A Collection of Performance Tasks and Rubrics:
Upper Elementary School Mathematics
Charlotte Danielson

Teaching, Learning and Assessment Together:
The Reflective Classroom
Arthur K. Ellis

Dedication

This book is dedicated to Howard Benjamin,
my wonderful husband.

Acknowledgments

I gratefully acknowledge the careful reading and constructive suggestions made by the following people: Kathy Bartley, Deborah Jagoda, Kim Sexton, Kathy Kelker, and Becky Kischnick. These educators help me immeasurably to adapt my ideas about differentiated instruction to the elementary level. I am grateful to Dawn Alcera for sharing her knowledge about teaching reading in science texts at Putnam Valley Elementary School. I continue to learn from my colleagues at Hendrick Hudson High school and from the members of the Assembly for the Teaching of English Grammar, an assembly of the National Council of Teachers of English. And, once again, I wish to thank Robert N. Sickles, my publisher, for his continued support and faith in me as I worked on this book.

Foreword

As an instructional coach, Amy Benjamin is the ultimate professional. She is direct, fair, informed, current, and insightful. Any teacher or administrator would be fortunate to have her courtside. The practical strategies and possible plans recommended in *Differentiated Instruction* are designed to help teachers revise their classroom performance. The result of this revision is ultimately tailored to increase student productivity and performance.

In an age of standards and testing, it is easy to lose sight of the long-term effect schooling can have on our learners. Every teacher knows there is a range of needs behind those faces staring up at them. Certainly, we need to help our students execute skill assessment well in formal testing situations, and Amy helps us here. What is impressive about her suggestions is that the teacher will enable students to see that the strategies and approaches they hone in class go beyond any test and can serve them in situations beyond the classroom. The key for the teacher is to provide what the individual student needs, to adjust classroom lessons accordingly, and to engage students in meaningful activity.

Amy Benjamin helps us see a way to take this formidable task on with intelligence and creativity.

Staff developers, curriculum writers, and instructors have much to value in these pages. Building on her previous work with Eye on Education, Amy is generating a productive set of books to coach us in this new century.

Heidi Hayes Jacobs

Meet the Author

My name is Amy Benjamin. I have been an English teacher at Hendrick Hudson High School in Montrose, New York, since 1973. I've taught all levels, all kinds of kids. Part of my job consists of working collaboratively with my colleagues and their classes on reading and writing in the content areas.

In addition to being a teacher, I am also, obviously, a writer of books such as this, and I run numerous workshops in New York and all around the country. Most of my workshops are about making kids better thinkers through the use of language. I've also written a couple of plays and a young adult novel. I tell you this because I know firsthand that there are different ways of being smart. When I was a student, school was a scary place, a place where I usually thought I was "doing it wrong." I'm left-handed, so I was awkward and backward at certain fine motor skills, such as handwriting and knitting. I have "my own system" of doing arithmetic. It works for me, but I thought I was cheating when I'd figure out that $26 + 8 = 34$ *because* I can picture two groups of fours added to 26. I'd make patterns like that in my head to help me add and subtract. I thought that was wrong to do, but I needed to do it. If no one had told my mother that she could teach me how to tie a bow by starting with two loops, I'd be wearing Velcro® sneakers today. I've always been considered "creative," but, to me, "creative" was just another way of saying that I couldn't follow directions.

Oh, and I'm also a union official for my New York State United Teachers local. I am responsible for conflict resolution and seeing to it that the collective bargaining agreement as well as proper labor practices are carried out.

I tell you these things about myself because I want you to know where my voice comes from. I'm a teacher, just like you. I take attendance, keep track of grades, call angry parents (as well as some appreciative ones), eat my lunch out of a thermal bag, go to staff development days, walk the talk from September to June. What I know about differentiated instruction is that:

- ◆ I've always done it, even before I knew it had a name.
- ◆ I could be better at it.
- ◆ It's important.

I hope that you find this information and the reflections enlightening and collegial. I wish you well in your professional quest to make learning real and lasting in your classrooms.

Table of Contents

How To Use This Book

This book is designed as a guide for elementary school teachers and administrators. We assume that you would like to make your classroom and school more responsive to the needs of children with a wide variety of learning styles, interests, goals, cultural backgrounds, and prior knowledge. The purpose of the text and discussion guides is to make you think, talk, question, apply new strategies, share effective practices, and improve what you already do well. This book is best used by colleagues who have convened in a course, a workshop, a staff development day, or some other forum in which reflection and revision of practice are possible.

1

Foundations

What Is Differentiated Instruction?

Across the country, the public is expecting more from educators. With nearly every state having a standards-based curriculum, *all* students are expected to achieve at a level higher than ever before. And that's good.

It's good because the standards movement has led to better staff development for teachers and administrators. Whereas in years past we might have been able to consign certain students to low-achieving classes, we now must find ways to make higher achievement accessible to everyone, no matter how challenging that is for all.

What do we mean by "higher achievement"? The Standards are about critical thinking skills, application of information, fluent and accurate use of the English language in written and oral expression, some exposure (later on) to a second language, and familiarity with a body of knowledge referred to as *cultural literacy*. Out of this goal of elevating the intellectual function of all students come the philosophy and the practice of differentiated instruction.

Context

Differentiated instruction is a broad term that refers to a variety of classroom practices that allow for differences in students' learning styles, interests, prior knowledge, socialization needs, and comfort zones. In most states, it involves a balance between the content and the competencies expected on the mandated assessments and various pedagogical options to maximize durable learning. The Standards tell us what students need to know and be able to do. Differentiated instruction practices help to get students there, while at the same time teaching them *how* to learn in a meaningful way.

In its modern application, a differentiated classroom is widely heterogeneous, dynamic, purposeful, and intense. The theory that guides differentiation is constructivism: *the belief that learning happens when the learner makes meaning out of information.* That may sound too self-evident to deserve mention. Of course, learning involves making meaning out of information. What else would learning involve? Well, if you've ever seen a kid memorize definitions for a list of "vocabulary words" without having the slightest idea of, nor any intention of learning, how to use those words in context, then you know what learning is *not*: We do *not* know the meaning of a word, the significance of a historical event, or the applications of a math process just because we have memorized a set of words. That is why the first step toward differentiated instruction is knowing what understanding means.

Why Now?

If Rip van Winkle were to wake up at the beginning of the 2000s and ask if there have been any changes in public education in the past generation, what would we tell him? We would probably start by telling him about the national imperative toward standardized testing. We would describe the intense pressures on administrators to produce test scores in their schools, making it appear that their schools outperform neighboring districts. These scores are going to be publicized in bar graphs in the local newspapers and even in real-estate offices. The better your kids and your neighbors' kids do on the state tests, the more your house will be worth. It's that simple.

But there's good news as well. In the 1990s, knowledge about the brain and learning burgeoned. Now, we know much more than we did 20 years ago about individual learning styles: how emotions and ambient conditions affect learning, how the mind processes and memorizes information, how important prior knowledge is, how various features of the classroom can enhance or impede learning, how the role played by the teacher/student relationship impacts student learning, how certain drugs can change one's ability to concentrate. The field of neurological science has delivered information which should have transformed the look and feel of classrooms across the country. How is all of our knowledge about learning actually being used to make students better learners? What is different in the actual delivery of service?

Reflection: Over Time

How has your practice changed since you began teaching? Consider as many internal and external factors as you can: *demographics, expectations, content, community relations, attitude, collegial relations, school climate, workload, materials, technology.*

Many factors would not appear to the naked eye. We would have to tell Rip about the litigiousness of the educational climate that we live in. We would tell him how special education regulations have created a paperwork system so Byzantine that the bureaucracy alone appears to defeat the intent of delivering instruction: Special education teachers are routinely pulled from their classrooms to attend meetings which are about filling out forms which are about why and how students aren't learning what they could be learning if the same teacher were only allowed to be teaching more and attending fewer meetings, reviews, evaluations, committees, and hearings.

Of course, Rip would see computers everywhere. How are they used? Do they enhance or do they diminish communication, information processing, curiosity, efficiency, understanding? With all this technology, Rip would surely assume that teachers, or, for that matter, everyone in this society, would have more time on their hands than they know what to do with. Do we have more leisure these days, or more work?

And we would have to tell Rip about Ritalin for ADHD and ADD, serotonin re-uptake inhibitors for depression and social anxiety, and other pharmacological marvels. If Rip found, as I believe he would, that our corridors and stairwells are more visibly disorderly than they've ever been, what forces would countervail those that would bring tranquility and learning readiness to our schools?

Reflection: School Climate

In the left column, list the policies and practices that have been put into place in the last 20 years in order to bring discipline and civility to our schools. In the right column, list the policies and practices that have accomplished the opposite effect. Consider as many societal factors as you can think of.

Dispelling Some Myths about Differentiated Instruction

In the education graveyard lie the bones of myths, fads, purist fanaticism, demagoguery, shallow thinking, and silliness. Is differentiated instruction (DI) just another passing fancy? Can we just watch the carousel go by until something we like better comes along? The answer is yes, if we look at DI simplistically, if we think there's a "recipe" for it, if we think that a half-day workshop or two is going to solve all our problems. The answer is no, if we understand that DI is a complex set of beliefs and practices that take respectful, humane, flexible principles of learning and human growth into account.

In conversations about education reform and at staff development sessions, we tend to hear clichés like these:

♦ *We're throwing the baby out with the bathwater:* Educators and people who care about education have a right to fear that in our zest to make education new and interesting rather than "drill and kill," we are abandoning basic skills. By *basic skills,* we mean reading, writing, clear speech, and computation, as well as the facts about history, geography, and science that schoolchildren are presumed to know. No one really has a definitive list of what these facts are and why everyone has to know them, but we get nervous when we think too many people don't know what the capital of North Dakota is.

♦ *We're reinventing the wheel:* This, like many of the other clichés, assumes that everything old is new again. The fact is that it's possible to make a better wheel, one that fits the kinds of cars that we drive now, rather than the covered-wagon wheels of yesterday. We do need to remember that not everyone is a veteran teacher. Some people, new to the field, are not reinventing the wheel but are discovering it. Some educators find no problem using the prepackaged teaching materials provided by textbook publishers. Others can't do that: They have to devise their own tests, performance tasks, and lecture notes. To the former, the latter is reinventing the wheel. (The capital of North Dakota is Bismarck.)

♦ *We've come full circle:* We're back to where we started. We're walking around in circles. Educators who lament that we've come full circle may think they would have been better off just by staying in the same place and waiting for the world to pass their way again. What they don't see is the value of the journey toward professionalism: To some, it may be a circle; to others, it's an upward spiral. Yes, here we are, with heterogeneous grouping instead of ability grouping again, or with the Redbirds and the Bluebirds again instead of heterogeneous grouping. But we haven't regressed unless we aren't bringing new skills and an enlightened attitude that learning is a complex process and that it isn't so easy to predict who is capable of learning what.

♦ *The pendulum has swung (will swing) the other way:* This either/or thinking is similar to the full circle thinking described above. It's usually said in a tone of vindication, meaning, "See? I didn't change my ways, and now I'm back in style, just like my powder blue tuxedo that I wore to my wedding." Or, "Why should I bother changing? If I wait long enough, this, too, shall pass." Actually, I don't think "it" will. We know too much about learning. I do think that the current mania for test scores won't last forever. I surely hope that the testing frenzy will abate, but I don't see Americans going back to the days when we gave up on kids as easily as we did in past generations. I don't think we're going to sort and classify kids into "college material" and "vocational school candidates" anymore. Nor do I think we will ever return to a golden age (that never existed) when kids and their parents treated the school with unquestioned deference. We're not going to reinstitute corporal punishment on a large scale. We *are* going to continue to humanize education and operate on the belief that every kid deserves to be taken seriously. If I didn't believe that, I wouldn't be doing this.

♦ *You can take a horse to water, but you can't make him drink:* This one is true enough, but it's too easy. As educators, we need to find out more about why the horse doesn't want to drink. We do have to assume that the horse might drink *eventually*, or maybe it would drink something that looked a little more appetizing. What this cliché means is that we absolve ourselves of the responsibility to do anything more than present material and give assignments. I have news for you: If that's all there is to our jobs, then we can be replaced by Web courses.

Reflection:
Understanding the Clichés

Consider the following questions in relation to differentiated instruction:
1. What's the baby, and what's the bathwater?
2. What is the wheel that keeps being reinvented?
3. Where does the full circle begin, and where does it end?
4. Where is the pendulum right now? In which direction is it swinging? How far do you think it will swing in this direction? What will make it start swinging in the other direction?
5. How do we get this stuff to look like something that the horse would drink?

Myth 1: Differentiated Instruction Consists of Students Doing Exercises in Self-Correcting Workbooks.

When I was a young teacher in the mid-1970s, something called "individualized instruction" was the fad. Students would come into a "reading" class, go for their folders, and then work themselves through various self-correcting exercises. The teacher would work quietly with students one at a time, perhaps "going over" problematical reading comprehension questions. These questions were based on isolated passages of the sort that might be found in a content area textbook. The level of difficulty of the workbook was color-coded.

The "individualized instruction" classrooms that I observed were dreary places. There was no student-to-student talk, no interest in the text, no joy of language, no classroom dynamic, no humor. Yet, this system was considered a breakthrough improvement over full class instruction.

I suspect that the term *differentiated instruction* evokes that image for many teachers, either because they once taught that way or because they were taught that way.

Myth 2: Differentiated Instruction Is the All-Purpose Problem Solver.

The techniques that you will read about in this book will make you a better teacher only if you use them the way you should use any pedagogy: in combination with others. No one method works all of the time for all students. Teachers have personalities, strengths and weaknesses, communication styles, and organizational habits. A particular pedagogy cannot be imposed on every teacher.

Myth 3: Differentiated Instruction Means That the Teacher Does Not Present Information.

Whole class presentations are an essential part of any effective teaching plan. There's no substitute for the modeling, enthusiasm, rich knowledge of subject, anecdotes, story-telling, and shared learning experience that an excellent teacher provides. Whole class instruction sets the tone, establishes the knowledge base, and ignites the interest of students. What it usually does not do is hold the individual accountable for making meaning out of the information. Performance tasks and communication do that.

Myth 4: Differentiated Instruction Does Not Work in Classes Where Students Have to Master a Body of Information for a High-Stakes Test.

Studies at reputable institutions have determined conclusively that *we can teach faster than kids can learn*. The implication here is that if we think we can "get kids through" the high-stakes test by "covering the curriculum" all by ourselves (without the help of the students), then we will find to our chagrin that we've accomplished nothing that the textbook couldn't have accomplished without us.

Myth 5: Differentiated Instruction Is Mainly for Students with Learning Deficits.

This myth presumes that DI practices are strictly remedial in nature, that they can only "slow down" students without learning deficits. First of all, I doubt that *anybody* is without a learning deficit: We all have our strengths and our weaknesses. When done well, DI enriches the learning of all students by engaging multiple intelligences, the arts, the emotions, and interdisciplinary connections.

Myth 6: Differentiated Instruction Means Dividing the Class into "Bluebirds" and "Redbirds."

A key to DI is flexible grouping, based on changing criteria: interests, prior knowledge, socialization skills, auditory comprehension abilities.

Myth 7: In a Heterogeneous Class, Brighter Students Will Be "Used" to Teach the Others.

I personally don't favor having students grade the papers of other students, "quiz" them orally, or be responsible to convey primary information. I don't even have a lot of faith in the "peer editing" phase of the writing process. I think there are better ways to teach revision. So, I don't believe that DI involves peer tutorials. There's a difference between cooperative learning and peer teaching. The former is based on constructing learning through socialization; the latter, in my opinion, makes an inappropriate request of students.

Myth 8: Differentiated Instruction Is a One-Room Schoolhouse Model.

"Does this mean I have to be Super-Teacher, devising multiple permutations of lessons to fit every kid all by myself?" DI implies team teaching, aide time, and assistance from in-house and itinerant specialists. The individual teacher in a self-contained class can't possibly do it all.

Myth 9: Once You Say You Have Differential Instruction, You'll Get All the Special Education Kids Thrown in.

The danger of being the kind of teacher who accommodates a wide variety of students is that sometimes those teachers are asked to do the impossible, or, certainly, that which is unfair. This is the "you can handle it" rule. DI should not result in the general ed teacher expected to be a special ed teacher.

Myth 10: Differential Education Is Cost-Free.

As we see from the above two explanations, yes, DI is expensive. Costs lie in aide time, specialists, consultants, smaller classes, differentiated materials and classroom accessories, technology, and time-out-of-class for teachers. You can't expect teachers to work with consultants, colleagues, and specialists and not be compensated, or be given time within the contractual day.

Myth 11: Differential Education Can Be Accomplished with a "Send and Fix" or "Send and Advance" Model.

You know the drill: Identify the kids who are "under," the ones who are "over," and send them out to a special place for islands of instruction. Rather than this, the regular classroom teacher needs a collaborative relationship with the remedial or enrichment specialists so that the "treated" students have something to contribute to the integral classroom agenda.

Reflection

Discuss the ideas in this section that you disagree with or that you think are unrealistic.

Values

Differentiated instruction is a practice that grows out of certain values. That is, the way we treat our students, design our curriculum, and establish rules depends upon what we think is important. Differentiated instruction requires planning, patience, organization, communication, and reflection. Consider the following statements and ask yourself if you agree with these values:

+ **The value of choice:** Students who have a choice in what they learn, how they learn it, and how they show what they know are more likely to experience real learning than students for whom the teacher makes all of the decisions.

+ **The value of learning how to learn:** In the process of learning, students should also be learning how to learn. This implies two-tiered teaching, that is, making students aware of *how* they learn as well as *what* they learn.

+ **The value of both ritual and variety:** The best classes are those that employ both ritual and variety in structure. Ritual is important because it establishes expectations, provides security, and instills trust that the teacher is in control. Although a routine can be a rut in which every day blurs into every other day, routine can also be a structure that allows us to memorize, because the routine provides cues that trigger memory of facts. Variety is also important. Variety can bring joy and excitement to learning. But the variety must exist within a ritualized structure for the learner to feel secure.

+ **The value of variety in assessments:** There are all kinds of ways to show what we know. As the teacher, you may use your discretion as to how different kinds of assessments are weighted into summative and formative grades, but your students are likely to be more successful if your assessment system takes in a broad spectrum of abilities and modes of expression.

+ **The value of collegiality:** Differentiated instruction thrives in a collegial community because you need ideas, encouragement, tips, a venue for reflection, and a wealth of sources. An increasing number of elementary classes with special education students are collaborative. Many schools use consultants to foster collegiality among teachers. Collaboration and sessions with consultants improve reliability, consistency of rules, and broadening of content and pedagogical knowledge. Collegiality, based on communication, is possible only when teachers have shared planning time. Shared planning time does not mean running into another fourth grade teacher in the copy room and asking if she's finished with the weather maps yet. Nor does having lunch together count as shared planning time. Shared planning time may take teachers away from their classrooms every few weeks as you and your colleagues convene to have serious, focused, businesslike discussions about professional concerns. Ideally, these sessions are presided over by a skilled consultant.

- **The value of student talk:** Effective classrooms are often highly interactive, dynamic, and communicative. However, this is not to say that there aren't times when it's the teacher who is doing the talking as the students listen and take notes or copy from the board.

- **The value of open-endedness:** "Closure" is not always necessary at the end of a topic. In traditional classes, the teacher "ties it up," but some methods of teaching, such as Socratic seminar, are purposefully left open-ended. The assumption is that thinking about the text should continue. Thinking doesn't always lead to knowing the answers. Sometimes, thinking leads to more questions.

- **The value of multiple learning modes:** The chances for durable learning are increased if there is a multiplicity of learning modes: imaginative, inquiry, facts, multisensory, technology, socialization.

- **The value of connection:** Students need to make connections to their own experience, interests, knowledge. This is why metaphors, anecdotes, and learning logs work well to effect durable learning. In fact, *any* connectedness has a positive learning effect: the relationship between teacher and student, the sense of community (or lack thereof) that the students feel in your classroom, the sense of connectedness that they feel to the school as a whole.

- **The value of different teaching styles:** Just as students have different learning styles, teachers have different teaching styles. Pedagogy is becoming increasingly scientific as we learn more about neurology and psychology. But it will never stop being an *art*, based on unquantifiable skills of communication, humor, intuition, hospitality, love of learning, and love of kids. You may be a teacher who relies on a textbook and a teacher's guide. Or, you may be someone who draws from a wide variety of primary sources. Your teaching style may be rich with language or rich with pictures. The point is that differentiated instruction for students does not put a crimp in the *teacher's* style. Rather, the ideas in this book offer you choices that you can adapt to your personality, beliefs, and strengths as a teacher.

Reflection

Which of the above statements do you disagree with? Why?

Personal Reflection

Think about the past week in your classroom. Which of the above statements would be evident? Do you think that more of these statements should be evident in your classroom?

Reflection:
What Does Your Class Look Like?

What *You* Are Doing:

- Writing on the board
- Grading papers while the kids watch a video
- Holding conferences with individual kids
- Holding conferences with small groups of kids
- Asking questions that you *do* know the answers to
- Asking questions that you *don't* know the answers to
- Explaining directions
- Going over homework or a test
- Telling personal anecdotes with direct relevance to the content
- Telling personal anecdotes with metaphorical relevance to the content
- Telling personal anecdotes to lighten the mood
- Reading aloud
- Taking attendance and performing record-keeping tasks
- Presiding over groupwork
- Explaining what is going to be on an upcoming test
- Referring to contemporary issues relevant to the content
- Explaining a visual
- Explaining and modeling a performance task
- Listening to student presentations
- Helping students plan their presentations
- Presiding over student writing
- Administering a test or quiz

- Leading a field trip
- Collecting and distributing
- Presiding over a library project
- Presiding over a research project involving in-class computers
- Tending to grooming and hygienic needs of individual children: "boots and button" lessons
- Tending to emotional needs of individual children
- Tending to social needs of individual children: teaching manners, resolving disputes
- Off-task behaviors

What the *Students* Are Doing:

- Copying notes from the board
- Watching a video
- Reading silently
- Taking a test or quiz
- Taking notes from a lecture where notes are not provided
- Talking with peers (on task)
- Constructing something
- Presenting something
- Asking close-ended questions
- Asking open-ended questions
- Answering close-ended questions
- Answering open-ended questions
- Going from picture to word
- Going from word to picture
- Telling personal anecdotes
- Listening to the teacher
- Listening to peers
- Being on a field trip
- Working at the computer
- Trying to put thoughts into words: written
- Trying to put thoughts into words: oral, for the teacher
- Trying to put thoughts into words: oral, for peers
- Organizing information
- Working in the library
- Finding information
- Off-task behaviors

In your own way, make a profile of your class in the last week. This could be a narrative, a discussion, a bar graph or other kind of graph, notes, or anything you choose.

If you are like every other teacher in the world, you can explain why your classroom is less than what you would like it to be. These explanations have nothing to do with you, of course. They have everything to do with students, parents, administrators, and society. If only students, parents, administrators, and society would cooperate, you would be the miracle worker. These explanations are called excuses. Let's get them out of the way right now:

- The students don't have a work ethic. They don't know what it is to delay gratification, to work toward a goal, to sacrifice.
- The students watch too much TV.
- Corollary: The students don't read.
- The parents excuse their children's irresponsible behavior.
- The school is expected to function more as an institution of social work than as an institution of learning.
- Students are excessively absent. They may be absent for whole days, or late, or called out of class. Your instructional time may be cut off because of an assembly or other special program.
- Parents and administrators make unreasonable demands.
- No one enforces rules. The school is chaotic.
- The kids get worse every year.
- The Administration doesn't give us what we need. They don't support us. They don't understand our needs. They don't care.

The reality of the above conditions is that they are only as real as you decide they are going to be. For every single one of these conditions, there's another way of looking at the situation. Yes, all of these conditions are annoying. If you let them overwhelm you, then you can add, "Teachers don't want to change the way they do things," to the list.

Maybe you are now wondering what you've gotten yourself into here. What does all this have to do with differentiated instruction? The relevance of the list of excuses is this: Differentiated instruction involves an attitude adjustment on *your* part. You can't change what goes on in your classroom until you clear away the excuses and do what needs to be done in spite of them. We won't accept excuses as excuses.

Learning to differentiate instruction means learning how to teach in a more informed way: a way that is open to reflection and adjustment, a way that will keep you busy enough to focus on solutions rather than problems.

The information in this books invites you to come to a better understanding of yourself as a teacher: your style, your values, your goals, your relationship with your students. You will think about your own uniqueness and needs, what you can do and what you can't, what you want to do and what you don't want to do. You are the key instrument of learning in your classroom: Students are affected by your beliefs and attitudes more than you may realize.

To differentiate instruction, you need to clarify the content (what you want students to know and be able to do), the process (how students are going to go about learning the content), and the product (how they will show what they know). Only when you know who you are deal with (yourself) can you then know how you can reach your students, with their diverse needs.

2

Where Do I Start?

In this chapter, you will learn how to assess your own teaching style, attitudes, and practices to clarify how you can refine your skills. You've already started differentiating instruction. You probably already do so more than you think. How have you incorporated any of the following practices in the last month? Think about:

- ♦ Your habits of mind
- ♦ The Big Ideas of thinking
- ♦ The Big Test
- ♦ Understanding your teaching style

Which of the following differentiated instruction (DI) practices do you already use?

- ♦ Flexible grouping
- ♦ Preassessment
- ♦ Interest centers
- ♦ Learning contracts
- ♦ Open reading choice
- ♦ Learning logs
- ♦ Reflective journals
- ♦ Inquiry and discovery
- ♦ Socratic seminar (text-based, open-ended, student-driven discussion)
- ♦ Portfolios
- ♦ Inclusion of the arts
- ♦ Allowing for readiness and prior knowledge
- ♦ Multisensory learning opportunities
- ♦ Learning opportunities that allow for multiple forms of intelligence
- ♦ Allowing for socialization
- ♦ Consideration of Bloom's taxonomy
- ♦ Multicultural considerations

Teacher Habits of Mind

Differentiated instruction results from certain habits of mind about teaching and learning. These habits of mind allow the teacher to be flexible in how she views her role. Consider the following.

As a teacher:

- ◆ **I revise and reflect:** In a differentiated classroom, teachers have the habit of mind to continuously rework, reword, and review lessons. The curriculum adheres to the demands of State Standards without becoming rigid. In order for student achievement to be lasting, teachers need to constantly ask themselves:

  - ◆ Is what the kids are doing meeting the Standards in terms of knowledge and skills?

  - ◆ Is my concern for individual differences working for or against my belief that students need to move outside their comfort zones?

  - ◆ Am I using both formal and informal means of assessment?

- ◆ I encourage lots of student talk: If differentiated instruction is constructivist, which it is, of course, then students need to talk the talk. A lot. They need to talk to each other, to the teacher, to themselves, in the language of the subject. Education reformer Heidi Hayes Jacobs urges teachers to "put words in kids' mouths." Just as learning a foreign language demands that the learner speak the new language, learning science, math, or history is learning a new language as well.

For some children, especially those from cultures other than American, the classroom is supposed to be a quiet place, where students are listening to the teacher. Such students are disturbed by the hubbub of student talk, and they even think that a noisy class is chaotic. This belief in student passivity, although unfounded, is widely respected and trusted. Many teachers feel out of control amid a lot of student talk. Indeed, it is easy for groups to get blown off course in a matter of seconds. Paradoxically, passive learning, where students are quiet receptors of teacher wisdom, is actually easier to manage than active learning. But modern differentiated instruction is not the old system of "coming in and getting your folders." If learning is to be constructed, it is to be constructed noisily.

- ◆ **I offer choices and alternatives:** A teacher who differentiates instruction has a larger vision of content, process, and assessment than one who does not. She believes not only that choices will make the students' work more interesting, but also that choices will make her own paperwork more varied. She believes that she can learn from her students.

- ◆ **I believe in reading:** When it comes to reading, like exercise, *quantity* matters. Reading plays a key role in all learning. Teachers who believe in reading are seen reading, owning and showing books, recommending books and articles, expecting students to read. Teachers who believe in reading welcome school-wide initiatives that encourage reading, even for token periods of time. Teachers who believe in reading model the joy of reading every chance they get: They refer to what they've read, they read aloud, they give and receive books as gifts, they visit bookstores frequently and talk about it.

- **I say, "This reminds me of . . . ":** This simple but powerful statement is the beginning of teaching students to learn by making connections to prior knowledge. By modeling this habit of mind, we invite students to make sense of new information.

- **I am interested in and curious about learning in general:** The habit of mind of "going beyond what is taught" is called *generative thinking*. The inspiring teacher models the behavior of the lifelong learner: visiting museums and cities, taking courses, joining discussion groups, taking part in civic affairs.

- **I value diversity:** Someone who values diversity learns about other cultures. She refers to various traditions, languages, and lifestyles. It's not very difficult to recognize the various ethnic groups in your classes and to ask questions, use examples, recommend readings, refresh your curriculum to make it inclusive.

- **I am aware of the networks, systems, and organization of knowledge:** To have this awareness is to be constantly making connections: connections to other fields of study, to contemporary issues, to popular culture, to the culture of the school and community, and to the students' and the teacher's personal lives. The stronger the network, the more durable the learning.

- **I practice professionalism:** To qualify as a professional, you have to be enthusiastic about intellectual growth. Professionals read widely, stay informed about public affairs, have well-grounded opinions. Professionals control their emotions in the workplace, adopting an attitude of service and humility.

- **I understand the cumulative nature of knowledge:** Traditional educators may conceive of learning in packaged "units." Although it is important to organize information around main topics, eras, themes, or regions, we close the door on long-lasting and meaningful learning with this "unit" thinking.

Reflection

Select *one* of these habits of mind that you would like to cultivate. Think of three actions that you can take to affect your classroom.

The Big Ideas of Thinking

Whatever the subject area, we are supposed to be teaching students how to think. We want them to think so that they can solve problems, adjust to new situations, make decisions, discern the important from the unimportant, protect themselves from those who would take advantage of them, appreciate traditions, express themselves, and understand others. The subject areas that we teach are the vehicles for improving our students' ability to think outside our classrooms.

In this chapter, I'll ask you to think about how the Big Ideas of thinking affect differentiated instruction. When students are processing course content through the lens of the Big Ideas, they are learning what to do with facts, just the way an artist learns what to do with colors.

There are various ways to categorize critical thinking skills. I'm naming them as follows:

- ◆ Comparison/contrast
- ◆ Connecting cause and effect
- ◆ Going from the generality to the specific, and back to the generality
- ◆ Justifying an assertion
- ◆ Understanding organization: arrangements, categories, subordination
- ◆ Description
- ◆ Evaluating against criteria

Comparison/Contrast

- ◆ How are seemingly like things different? (making fine distinctions)
- ◆ How are seemingly different things alike? (making connections)

You may never have thought of it this way before, but almost all learning involves comparison/contrast: the ability to distinguish sameness and difference. Suppose you are teaching about recycling in the household. Have students generate questions that compare and contrast different materials:

- ◆ Distinguish between organic and non-organic materials.
- ◆ What categories do non-organic materials fall into?
- ◆ What materials fall into more than one category? How do we determine how to recycle these?
- ◆ What are the differences and similarities between any two categories, such as glass and metal?
- ◆ Trace the recycling journey.
- ◆ Make a poster that shows people how to recycle their household products.
- ◆ Make a list of 10 new words that you have learned about recycling.
- ◆ What would be three ways that you could improve your recycling habits? (Compare what we do to what we *could* do.)

- What consumable items can you reduce?
- What consumable items can you re-use?
- What consumable items can you re-program (use an item for a different purposes, rather than discarding it)?

This kind of examination of similarities and differences is differentiated instruction because students are free to interpret the question in various ways, with more sophisticated students envisioning finer distinctions.

Connecting Cause and Effect

Understanding causes and effects is a sophisticated critical thinking skill. A cause and effect word bank includes: *therefore, thus, so, as a result, consequently.* Have students compose sentences using this word bank to discuss recycling and conservation.

This approach to making meaning of the ecology consciousness topic is differentiated instruction because not everyone's sentences are expected to be the same. Putting all of these sentences together for the class would be a powerful lesson.

Going from the Generality to the Specific, and Back to the Generality

This can be done through an hourglass outline:

Generality:_____

    Supportive detail:_____

    Supportive detail:_____

    Supportive detail:_____

Generality:_____

Justifying an Assertion

An assertion can be an opinion, a claim, a generality, anything that is set forth as truth. Novices are often at a loss for words to justify their opinion. Consider the following assertions about recycling:

- Recycling costs more than it is worth.
- Deciding whether or not to recycle should be up to the individual.
- We should do more recycling in our school.

Understanding Organization: Arrangements, Categories, Subordination

Finding patterns is an essential meaning-making skill. Students can express patterns in various ways: graphic organizers, outlines, paragraphs and essays, lists, color-coded text markings. To incorporate differentiated instruction, have the students develop their own categories, rather than laying out the main headings. For recycling, some categories that students come up with might surprise you:

- New inventions
- Famous people
- Diseases and troubles
- What I like
- What I don't like
- Famous events
- Stories about it

Description

A good description involves precise and lively language, attention to detail, spatial organization, transitional words, and variety. Have students consider a particularly vivid and multifaceted scenario that represents ecological issues, and have them describe it in either words or pictures.

Evaluating Against Criteria

Bloom's taxonomy places evaluation at the highest level of thinking, because evaluation takes into account content knowledge as well as comparison/contrast, synthesis, and analysis. If you ask students to formulate questions about ecological matters they might ask:

- Would you consider conservation and recycling a reason to vote for someone?
- What else can we do in our classroom, schools, home, and community to educate people about the importance of conservation and recycling?
- What are some reasons why people don't recycle as much as they could?
- Does the habit of recycling save, or cost, your family money?

Evaluating against criteria also refers to engineering: when you consider how to build a structure, you have criteria: it must withstand certain forces and stresses, serve a particular function, and meet practical limitations such as size and cost.

Reflection

1. Use the Big Ideas of thinking to compose essential questions for a unit of study. Consider the subject as a whole rather than as a smaller unit. Consider interdisciplinary applications.

2. Use the Big Ideas of thinking to compose differentiated performance tasks.

3. Use these criteria to evaluate your performance tasks in Reflection 2 above:

- ♦ The task depends upon the content that I want students to learn. They need to use generalities as well as details. They could not do this task if they hadn't been in my class.
- ♦ The task list provides for differentiation in terms of student choice, interests, readiness, and learning styles.

The process of doing this task will help students to remember and apply the course content.

- ♦ By doing this task, students will learn a particular part of the course content better than they would have through a traditional test alone.
- ♦ Doing this task is likely to bring about better results on a traditional test.

Differentiated Instruction for the Big Test

We live in the day of the Big Test. Every state in the nation (except Iowa) has Standards and Assessments, and these S&A's typically culminate in the BTE (Big Test Experience). Whenever I work with teachers on critical thinking skills, reading and writing, and differentiated instruction, they want to connect their pedagogy to the Big Test.

In today's educational climate, The Big Test reigns supreme. No question about it. Your school district, building, even you, as an individual teacher, are measured up (sometimes publicly) against your colleagues in terms of "how your kids did on the Big Test." You will pay dearly if you frittered away time figuring out how to get students involved, interested, engaged at the "expense of covering material" for the BT.

Reflection

Do you agree or disagree with the following statements:
1. The Big Test accurately assesses the Standards in all subject areas.
2. Having the Big Test has improved student achievement and the teaching profession.

Tiered Performance Tasks

We think of tiered performance tasks as tri-leveled tasks (low, middle, high) assigned to students after a preassessment is done to determine who belongs at which of the three levels. Although they call for varying degrees of depth and complexity, these tasks are designed to "look the same" when handed out to the students. They may be color-coded.

Differentiated instruction is not about having bright students do "more" or "harder" work just because they "can handle it." It works best when students who find depth and complexity in a topic or text are given the freedom to do so, while students on a less sophisticated level can work accordingly. In a tiered performance task, the content is the same. You start with a group lesson or text. Then you present the choices, or you can match up student to task as appropriate. You may want to give students time to try their hand at all three tasks before they make their choices.

Figure 2.1 illustrates an interdisciplinary tiered task that grew out of a fifth grade pullout program for gifted and talented students. The task was re-designed to be brought back into the classroom for all students, as a tiered task to accommodate different learning levels.The text is a children's story entitled "The Wump World" by Bill Peet (Houghton Mifflin). It is an allegory that leads us to think about endangered species. (Note that quality children's literature can be read on many levels and is accessible to students of varying abilities.)

Figure 2.1. The Endangered Species Report

Tier I. Write a report that gives the following information about the endangered species that you have selected. Each section should have a heading. Each section should have one to three well-developed, complete sentences. Here are your topics:

- **Species:** Give the full scientific name, as well as what ordinary people (not scientists) call this animal.
- **Habitat:** Describe the environment where your animal lives.
- **Why Endangered:** Explain the things happening in the environment that are endangering your animal.
- **Projections:** Show how scientists predict that the numbers of this animal will decrease over the years. Use math to express this information.
- **Course of action to prevent extinction:** Using your knowledge of science and how our government makes things happen, suggest at least one course of action that will save this animal from extinction.
- **Consequences:** Use your knowledge of science to predict what might happen (and why) if and when this animal becomes extinct.

Tier II: Write a letter to the editor of your local newspaper which explains why your animal is an endangered species, why people should care about this, and what you want the government and individuals to do to prevent extinction. Use a serious and persuasive tone. Use facts and numbers.

Tier III: Act as if there is a Congressional hearing to present arguments that would protect your animal. You have two minutes to address the committee. Using notes, visuals, facts, and statistics, present your case. This is an oral report; your notes will be collected.

For all three tasks, you must submit a bibliography with at least three sources.

Contracts

Learning contracts are similar to tiered performance tasks in that students have a choice in what they do. The difference is that with a learning contract, students decide on the quantity of work that they wish to do in exchange for an agreed-upon grade. The contract must be in writing, with consequences for late or unsatisfactory performance clearly spelled out.

One of the drawbacks of learning contracts is that some students will complete their contracts earlier than others, and then be unproductive and distractive in class. You can offer extra credit, supplemental readings, library time, or computer time, but these "solutions" will not be attractive to the student who has rushed through the contract so that class time could be "free." If too many students end up with spare time, then the contract system needs to be improved, or more work should be expected to be done outside the classroom.

Arriving at a good, functional learning contract is not as easy as it would appear.

Let's say that you set aside a week of in-class time for students to fulfill their contracts. A child's sense of time is not the same as yours. Children need assistance with schedules. They can monitor their progress with a daily check-off sheet. You also need to make a plan for absences, technical glitches, lack of availability of the librarian or other specialists, and other obstacles that will thwart the contract. You may want to set the due date for Thursday, with Friday as a "grace" day. This method of differentiated instruction is not for the novice teacher.

Compacting

Compacting the curriculum is a strategy that works best for math, grammar, and spelling. Based on a preassessment, students are excused from "learning" material that they have demonstrated mastery on. They are accelerated to their instructional level. Often, this is where a learning contract will come in, where the advanced student works independently. It is important that these students not be "excused" from homework. They may choose homework from another source, such as a list of supplemental readings or an advanced workbook.

Not every student who has aced the pretest jumps at the chance to do harder work. If a higher grade is not on the table, it's probably unrealistic to expect students to pedal harder. The reward of either higher grades or less homework has to be part of the deal.

Reflection

Teachers brainstorm and discuss all of the problematical issues concerning grading policies and procedures, such as the ones that are given in this chapter.

- ◆ **Flex:** Make a list of all of the activities that students could use for discretionary points in your class.

- **Class Participation:** Make a rubric for class participation that delineates specific manifestations of productive participation.
- **Leadership:** What opportunities for student leadership exist in your classroom?
- **Tiered Performance Tasks:** Transform a performance task into a three-tiered task. Consider the whole class lesson that the task would be based on. Evaluate your tiered performance task as follows:
    - Would the students consider each task comparable in terms of the time and effort that it would take to do them?
    - Do the tasks take into account student learning styles, interest, prior knowledge, and readiness?

Understanding Your Teaching Style: How Will Differentiated Instruction Work for You?

Teachers entering into differentiated instruction must begin by understanding their own teaching styles, learning styles, personality types, and strengths and weaknesses. They must know what people in the investment world call their "tolerance for risk." By making your instruction more differentiated, you may feel that you are taking a risk. If you are used to feeling in control by knowing what everyone is doing, how they are doing it, and when and how they will show what they know, then you may have to start thinking of yourself as someone who is in control in a different way.

We will be working with three statements. In order to proceed with DI, you need to understand what these statements mean to you and how they are reflected in your classroom. You need to consider how these statements describe your classroom right now and how they describe the classroom that you are striving to have.

1. **Knowledge and Skills Are Actively Created, Rather Than Passively Learned**
    - Explain what this statement means to you.
    - What is going on in your classroom when knowledge and skills are actively created? Give a specific example. Is this working to effect the desired learning outcomes? How do you know?
    - What is going on in your classroom when students are passively learning? Is this working to effect the desired learning outcomes? How do you know?
    - What are the challenges for the teacher in a class where students are actively learning? How have you been successful? What issues remain problematical for you?

2. **In Delivering Instruction and in Assessing Students, Teachers Need to Consider Individual Differences**
    - Make an exhaustive list of how students in your class might have individual differences.
3. **Learning Is Affected by Social and Emotional Conditions**
    - Do you agree with this statement? If so, can you give examples from your own learning?
    - What social and emotional conditions do you have control of in your classroom? What social and emotional conditions do you have no control over?

3

The Language of Differentiated Instruction

Because differentiated instruction is broad-based, much of the language used to discuss it are terms heard elsewhere in educational conversation. Presented here are some thumbnail working definitions to help you navigate though this book.

Academic literacy: Academic literacy is the ability to efficiently read academic texts. Academic literacy differs from the literacy that is required to read fiction. When we read fiction, we usually do so for pleasure, looking to lose ourselves in the beauty of the language and the story. With academic readings, we need to employ strategies of reading that are directed more toward finding specific information and remembering it.

A child who is learning academic literacy is learning how to:

- Locate information in a textbook by using the table of contents and index
- Use a glossary
- Skim for main ideas
- Scan for specific facts
- Study from a textbook
- Outline information
- Use multiple sources to answer a question or pursue a topic
- Locate information in the library
- Use various print and on-line reference tools
- Locate and interpret maps
- Interpret graphs and other nonprint layouts
- Organize data
- Evaluate the validity and applicability of sources

Adjusted questioning: When a teacher practices adjusted questioning, she alters the depth, complexity, and need for prior knowledge to accommodate the children in the class. Some children may require direct, literal questions; others are ready for questions requiring abstractions. Adjusted questioning is one way to achieve a level of differentiation in whole class instruction.

Alternative assessments (aka authentic assessments, performance tasks): Alternative assessments are ways, other than the traditional "pencil and paper" tests, for students to show what they know. Written reports can be considered alternative assessments when they are something other than traditional essays or straightforward "reports" (which are usually not good assessments anyway, since they are so easily plagiarized). Many teachers bring in the various forms of intelligence when drawing up alternative assessments. In teaching writing for social communication, a teacher might have students write thank you notes or invitations. For science, it might be caring for a plant or pet and keeping a log of its needs and progress. Art and music are based almost entirely on authentic assessment.

Here are some questions that will help you recognize authentic assessment:

♦ Does the task arise from the need to solve a real problem?

♦ Does the task require planning, communication, research, or cross-disciplinary thinking?

♦ Is the task memorable?

♦ Did the student have any input into the nature of the task?

♦ Can the task be evaluated against a rubric?

♦ Does the task have real-world connections?

♦ Will every student produce the same exact product?

♦ Is the task completed over time?

♦ Will the task enable the student to better understand her own learning needs?

♦ Will the task capitalize on the student's strengths and strengthen her weaknesses?

It is not necessary for a task to meet all, or even most, of these questions to be considered authentic. The key is that authentic assessments give the student a sense of ownership of the learning and the product, whereas inauthentic tasks have the feel of "doing something for the teacher." A spelling test, for example, based on a given list of words that seems random to the students, would be considered an inauthentic task. To assess spelling authentically, you would have to look at how students spell the words that they are actually writing, how they form patterns among words, and whether they at least have a logical, phonetic approach to spelling.

Anchor activities: Anchor activities are activities that children can do by themselves: reading a book-of-choice, writing in their journals, keeping learning logs, using graphic organizers, reviewing and reinforcing material that needs to be memorized. Typically, children have anchor activities to do at their own desks or in the Quiet Corner.

Bloom's taxonomy (often referred to as "Bloom"): When educators say "Bloom," they are referring to six levels of learning, from most basic (knowledge) to most sophisticated (evaluation). Bloom's taxonomy establishes this hierarchy:

1. *Knowledge:* The learner has the information. She knows the cast of characters in her state capital.

2. *Comprehension:* The learner understands the information. She understands what her legislators and state committees can do.

3. *Application:* The learner can use the information. She can write to her state representatives, expressing her opinion or asking for assistance on appropriate matters.

4. *Analysis:* The learner can take apart and put together the information. She can identify the parts of a particular problem that could be solved by action by the state legislature. She can understand and proceed on their response.

5. *Synthesis:* The learner can bring together disparate information. Having received a response from her legislator, she can propose another solution based on information from another source. She can devise creative solutions.

6. *Evaluation:* The learner can make judgments based on criteria. She can compare and contrast various solutions, and can decide which is best in terms of cost, feasibility, popularity, environmental impact, and other factors.

Some teachers differentiate instruction according to the taxonomy. They may begin every task with a "Bloom verb." If students were learning about the solar system, the hierarchy of learning might look like this:

Level 1: Name the nine planets and give one fact about each. Decide what kinds of facts you want to give. You may decide to give facts about size, distance from the sun, distance from Earth, number of satellites (moons), where the planet got its name.

Level 2: Explain why we have night and day and seasons of the year.

Level 3: Write a story for a kindergarten class about the phases of the moon. In your story, explain the phases of the moon using words that a kindergarten class can understand.

Level 4: Draw a model of the solar system showing where the planets are at this time of year in their orbit and where they will be three months from now.

Level 5: Read about global warming. Make a presentation to the class that explains why global warming might or might not be happening. You may work with a partner and present your report as a debate. Be sure to use facts.

Level 6: Suppose there were a movie about a planet that goes out of orbit and threatens to crash into Earth. Explain why you think this is or is not possible. What would have to happen to make this movie come true?

Brain-based learning: (aka brain-compatible learning): This is a way of looking at how learning results from the integration of prior knowledge, emotions, physical comfort or discomfort, nutrition, attitude, patterns, frameworks, the arts, interdisciplinary thinking, habits of mind, expectations, and culture. Learning, a human activity, is the result of all that we feel and experience in the learning context. Teachers who are trained in brain-based learning consider how the brain memorizes and retrieves information, how we apply what we learn, and how we can enrich the ambience so that the learning is long-lasting. The teacher who has a classroom biology center, consisting of live animals and plants for children to care for is creating a knowledge base for facts about science to "stick onto."

The principles of brain-based learning that play into differentiated instruction are these, as extracted from the work of Caine and Caine (1997):

1. The All-at-Once Effect: If the brain were a machine, we could call it a parallel processor. This means that we think, emote, imagine, and perceive all at the same time. We are "in the moment." As teachers, the simultaneity of learning means that students need multisensory input: texts, graphics, video, charts, audio, dialogue, on-line research, and interpersonal interactions to learn complicated material. The more sensory input the learner has, the more likely she is to form connections that will strengthen memory and comprehension.

   In addition to these orchestrated learning conditions, the learner is simultaneously affected by stress, hunger, nutrition, lighting, state of comfort, background noise. While it is true that we can't serve breakfast, control the weather, be personal trainers, tuck kids into bed at a reasonable hour, or chase after kids with a spoonful of cough medicine, we do need to think of teaching as an act of *hospitality.* Like hosts, we invite kids in, make them feel welcome, interesting, and valued. Differentiating instruction means making kids feel that they are *interesting.* Through their own interests, they can learn what we offer.

2. The Natural Search for Meaning: The human brain seeks to make sense, to create order out of chaos. To make sense of things, we categorize, name, connect. We practice the Sesame Street[R] game of "One of These Things Is Not Like the Other." We find sameness and difference. Think about how important this is. It is through discerning similarities and differences that we make meaning out of

almost everything we know. We generalize one case to another, find exceptions, figure out where new things belong, define concepts, apply rules and bend them, all based on how we figure out what is the same and what is different.

3. Pattern-Finding: An extension of the "same and different" search for meaning is that the brain makes meaning by finding patterns, by seeking an organizing principle. A pattern is a repeating and predictable cluster. An organizing principle is a rule that governs how a pattern is put together.

4. Emotions and Pattern-Finding: Not surprisingly, the patterns we discover parallel emotions that we are experiencing. Perhaps we are feeling emotions based on experiences of separation, fear of the unknown, joy, or relief. We may view the world through that lens. To differentiate instruction, we need to show students how to use their emotions to find patterns and make connections.

5. Simultaneous Processing of Parts and Wholes: One of the fiercest controversies of the past two decades in education is between phonics and whole language instruction. A related controversy involves "writing process" versus "explicit grammar instruction." Both sides are about the relationship between the parts and the whole. But when we encamp ourselves too firmly on one side or the other, we fail to understand that the brain processes part and whole simultaneously. The best research on reading and writing instruction favors an integrated, differentiated approach, wherein the student learns both the parts (phonics) and the whole (language in context) simultaneously. This is how musicians and athletes have always learned their crafts.

6. The Role of Peripherals: While students are learning the main event, they are also learning from the visuals around them, side conversations and background noise, and other input from the edges of the learning environment. The mind picks up peripheral words and thoughts and brings them to the foreground.

7. Challenge and Threat: Challenge enhances learning; threat inhibits learning. We learn best when we feel safe. When threatened, the learner retreats, marshaling self-protective defenses, going into a nonproductive mode.

Choice boards: Choice boards are charts with pockets to stock task cards. The task cards are arranged in an order that the teacher determines: by skill and readiness levels, by subject, by learning styles or multiple intelligence, by time frames (how long it may take to complete a task).

Chunking of information: This term is often used to refer to the brain's search for meaningful relationships, patterns, connections. New information needs something to stick to: It must stick to *known* information. We can exploit this brain fact in how we teach seemingly isolated facts, such as spelling. Some visuals that facilitate chunking of information are graphic organizers, color coding, Velcro and magnet boards.

Clustering: Clustering is a technique of prewriting to formulate groups of related ideas which can later be developed into formal writing. Clustering can also be used as a study technique. It is an effective way of making new information stick to known information. Using clustering as a prewriting/brainstorming technique offers a means of subordinating supportive ideas to key ideas.

Compacting (aka curriculum compacting): This term refers to eliminating from the curriculum information and skills that a student has already mastered. Based on a preassessment, the teacher advances students to their instructional level. Compacting is popularly used in math classes. The danger of this pedagogy is that we don't want advanced learners to feel that they are "being given more work." Nor do we want some students to feel that they are being sent off on their own. Compacting can work for short periods of time, when students are given choices about what to do with their classtime once they have shown mastery on a given topic. In a math class, the teacher may wish to preassess for mastery on rate/time/distance word problems. Upon determining who already understands the concept, the teacher can have advanced students make up their own word problems based on actual airline schedules. Teachers who use compacting often send letters home to parents explaining the rationale, procedures, and expectations.

Constructivism: (aka active learning): This is the idea that learning is not passively received but actively constructed by the learner. Differentiated instruction is a constructivist practice. Constructivist practices emphasize use of background knowledge, authentic assessment, metacognition, and use of technology.

Content, process, product: In the language of differentiated instruction promoted by Carol Ann Tomlinson (ASCD), we often hear these terms. Differentiating content means that students will be learning different information about the same topic. A science class learning about oceanography may differentiate *content* by having four groups of students choose among four topics: measurements, tidal patterns, marine biology, and the ocean floor. Another class may have all of the students learn about ocean measurements by means of whole class instruction, and then differentiate *process* if some students make a color-coded chart, others construct a model, and others make an outline of information from the textbook chapter. To differentiate *product*, students could choose between a written report, an oral report, or a traditional short answer test to show what they know.

Cultural capital: This term refers to the "outside of school" self. It includes dialect, socioeconomic status, family attitudes and expectations, exposure to reading material, travel, sense of safety and well-being. Because of the importance of prior knowledge, cultural capital is an extremely important learning factor. Field trips, in-house performances, technology, multicultural education and student exchanges all enhance cultural capital and build learning capacity.

Curriculum components: The three components of curriculum are information (content), skills, and assessment. Another way of looking at curriculum is: *What concepts and competencies are you learning, and how will you show what you know?*

Deductive reasoning: Deductive reasoning is reasoning that begins with a general rule and then goes into specifics based on that general rule. Direct instruction, where the teacher delivers a body of knowledge, usually depends upon deductive reasoning on the part of the students: The teacher gives the generality, such as a spelling rule, and the students apply it to specifics.

Depth and complexity: When we differentiate instruction for content, we think in terms of how to adjust depth (going into more or less detail in a narrower field) and complexity (having more steps, making more connections, having more interrelated parts). For example, in a second grade class learning about the President of the United States, depth would involve achieving an understanding of some of the jobs that the President does; complexity would involve beginning to understand that there are three branches of government and where they do their work.

Dialectical journal (aka a double-sided journal): The dialectical journal is the student's "conversation with herself" regarding a reading. On the left side, the student summarizes the reading. On the right side, she writes affective or interpretive responses. These can include questions, "this reminds me of . . . " statements, vocabulary lists, predictions, agree/disagree statements, further examples. The newspaper or student-selected outside reading works well with the dialectical journal.

Emotional intelligence: Emotional intelligence refers to a person's ability to function well in social situations, especially stress-producing ones. Emotional intelligence involves communication skills, self-control, perceptiveness to the needs and concerns of others, self-understanding, and intuition. Timing, humor, empathy, and patience are characteristics of emotional intelligence. Contrary to outdated beliefs, emotional intelligence can be learned.

Embedded application: Embedded application occurs when a skill, such as recording measurements, is an integral part of a learning task, such as writing a lab report.

Entry points: This term comes from Howard Gardner's work on multiple intelligence. Gardner (1991, 1993) names five "entry points," or pathways, to learning a given topic: *narrational* (entering the topic via a story), *logical/quantitative* (entering the topic via numbers, deductive reasoning, or scientific inquiry), *foundational* (entering the topic via its philosophy or key words), *aesthetic* (entering the topic via the arts), and *experiential* (entering the topic via physical contact, by manipulating the objects and materials involved).

Features of differentiation: Differentiated instruction can be about any or all of the following: *pacing, degree of structure that the teacher provides, degree of* *independence of the learner, number of facets in the learning task, level of abstractness or concreteness, and level of depth and complexity.*

Flexible grouping: Flexible grouping is a key practice of differentiated instruction. Groups can be formed in various ways: interest, self-selection, or random. What we *don't* want is the formation of groups that are obviously ability-based. Such grouping is humiliating to the low-functioning group and breeds arrogance and a sense of entitlement in the "smart group." Cooperative learning groups work best when roles are clearly assigned. One popular method is based on "literature circles." In a literature circle, each member of the group has a job to do: word looker-upper, metaphor-finder, illustrator, title-maker, connector.

Graphic organizer: A graphic organizer, also called a concept map or web, is any kind of diagram or outline that helps the learner to arrange information visually. The Harvard outline and the sentence diagram are graphic organizers which have been around for more than a hundred years to help learners. The trouble is, the graphic organizer can become so complicated that it becomes its own taskmaster. Popular graphic organizers are the Venn diagram for comparison/contrast, the Frayer model for concept attainment, the KWL chart for reading comprehension, and the flow chart for sequential information.

Inclusion classes: Often called "collaboration classes," this is a model in which students with special needs are taught within the regular class, along with a special education teacher who works collaboratively with the subject area teacher. There are various models of inclusion. Sometimes, the special education teacher is present for every class; other times, she may work with mainstream classes in two subject areas, alternating from one to the other. Sometimes, the special education teacher and her class work as a separate class most of the time, merging with the mainstream classes for appropriate projects. For collaboration to work, teachers need training, common planning time, opportunity for reflective practice and lots of communication and administrative support.

Inductive reasoning: Inductive reasoning is reasoning that begins with the specifics and draws generalities based on them. A detective gathering information about a crime uses inductive reasoning to draw a conclusion about what happened.

Inquiry activities: Reading specialists refer to such activities as the KWL chart as an inquiry activity. The reader establishes overt goals for the reading, sets up expectations, makes predictions, and self-monitors her reading, aware of what she is looking for in the text.

KWL chart: This popular and effective three-column chart stands for "know, want to know, learned." Here's how it works: Before reading, the student jots down what she already knows about the subject. In the second column, she writes what she wants to know. After the reading, in the third column, she writes what she's learned. This marshals prior knowledge and focuses the reading. The KWL comports with everything we know about effective reading. It should be used in every class.

Learning centers: With learning centers, the room is physically arranged so that students interested in a particular type of learning can congregate. Centers can be oriented around activities, readings, topics, themes. Learning centers work well with contracts. In a sixth grade social studies class learning about ancient Greece, students turned the classroom into a museum. The groups created stations based on philosophy, government, theater, and architecture. Each station had student-designed activities, which the class completed by rotating around the room.

Learning contracts: Learning contracts are written agreements between teacher and student stipulating that certain learning tasks will be carried out by a certain time. A contract is a *negotiated agreement* between two sides. When a teacher hands out an assignment and declares that it is due by her deadline, that is *not* a learning contract. The student must have a part in drawing up the terms of the contract. In a creative writing class, the teacher and the student could discuss the nature of the writing project (making a short story out of a poem), the length, interim due dates, and criteria for evaluation.

Learning logs: A learning log is a general term for some sort of notebook in which the learner will track her own learning. Entries can include questions, predictions, graphic organizers, summaries, mnemonic devices, connections to real life and other subject areas, diagrams, and vocabulary lists. KWL charts and dialectical journals are often part of the learning log.

Learning profile: This refers to a student's preferred methods for learning: learning style, sensory strengths, interests, aptitudes, deficits.

Learning style: A person's learning style is her best way of processing, remembering, and using information. We usually think of learning style in terms of the senses: visual learners, auditory learners, kinesthetic learners. Some people learn best by socializing; others, by writing; others, by talking to themselves aloud. We speak of brain laterality: the right hemisphere is the realm of intuitive learning; the left, of quantitative learning. Special education teachers are experts in adapting information to a student's best **learning** style. Effective learners have a keen understanding of their own learning styles.

Microskills and macroskills: Microskills are skills in isolation, such as the skill of arranging things in order. Macroskills are microskills used in combination. Problem solving calls for macroskills.

Multiple intelligence theory: Developed by Howard Gardner, the multiple intelligence theory posits that there are eight different kinds of intelligence. These are verbal-linguistic, musical-rhythmic, logical-mathematical, interpersonal, intrapersonal (knowing of the self), bodily-kinesthetic, visual-spatial, and naturalistic (understanding the natural world). Multiple intelligence theory plays an important role in differentiated instruction.

Orbitals: Often used for advanced students, orbitals are independent studies that the students work on for several weeks. The student selects her own topic, a "spin-off" from what the rest of the class has worked on and what it will be working on while the student does the independent work. Students work through orbitals with coaching from their "home base" teacher, as well as from librarians, computer specialists, and other specialists.

Portfolios: Portfolios are organized collections of evidence of learning over time. There are all different types of portfolios. A portfolio differs from a folder with papers stuffed in it, in that a portfolio represents a carefully selected array of work samples that show goals, growth, and introspection. Portfolios are just as valid whether they represent an entire school year or one particular area of study. They are an excellent way of differentiating instruction and are limited only by your imagination.

Problem-based learning: Students solve problems in much the same way that adults do on their jobs. The teacher presents students with an unclear, complex problem, and the students use a group process to solve the problem. The problem could be real (improving the recycling habits of the school and community) or hypothetical (what problem is the President of the United States trying to solve right now?).

Scaffolding: As the metaphor implies, scaffolding is a support system for learning. The purpose of a scaffold device is to allow the learner to build new information upon a foundation of prior knowledge. Scaffolds can be graphic organizers, short-answer questions, dialogue, word banks, and other learning supports.

Schema: A schema is an organizational framework of knowledge upon which new knowledge can be built. Having a schema allows us to mentally fill in details and make assumptions about whatever it is that we are learning. The more sophisticated the learner, the more elaborate is the schema that she brings to the body of knowledge being learned. We hear a lot about schemas in differentiated instruction pedagogy. The reason is that any student's ability to learn new information will be based on the richness of the schema that she brings to the subject. Assessing the detail and accuracy of a student's schema for a particular topic is one way of preassessing.

Semantic maps: Semantic maps are graphic representations of vocabulary. One kind of semantic map is the "Yes/No/Maybe" model in which the student writes the name of a concept, such as "civilizations," at the head of the paper. She then sorts various words in the yes/no/maybe columns, depending on whether they are civilizations, not civilizations, or ambiguities. Other forms of semantic maps show related words, etymology trees, synonym/antonym lists, characteristics or elements of the concept. The value of the semantic map is that it calls for critical thinking about what a concept name really means.

"Show what you know" assessments: "Show what you know" assessments are demonstrations of the student's knowledge in a form that is chosen by the student. The student makes a proposal, describing how her project will display her knowledge. She may offer to make up a short-answer or an essay test, make an oral or a written report, do a creative project. One caveat: The product cannot be something that can be taken in whole from another source. It should have enough of an in-class component that the teacher sees the product being constructed.

Socratic seminar: A Socratic seminar is a student-centered, open-ended discussion based on a text. The text may be print or nonprint. The purpose of a Socratic seminar is to invite conversation that is grounded in textual information. A Socratic seminar does not end in closure because its purpose is to stimulate independent thought rather than to come to any particular conclusion. The teacher's role in a Socratic seminar is to ask questions and direct the students to focus on the text for their answers.

Textual features: Textual features are the visual cues that assist reading comprehension, especially in textbooks. Textual features that are helpful to the reading process are writing in columns, pictures, graphics, headings, bold-faced and italic type, introductory and chapter-end questions. Textual features help the reader scan for specific information, and they direct the reader's attention to key points.

Tiered assignments: Tiered assignments, usually presented on three levels, are tasks constructed with different levels of depth and complexity in mind. Some teachers use preassessment to determine which students are best suited to which tier. Others rely on student choice.

Think-pair-share: This is a cooperative learning strategy in which students are given a question and then asked to think about the answer, discuss their thoughts briefly with a partner, and then share the fruits of their discussion with others.

Transcendent thinking modes: These are ways of analyzing, synthesizing, comparing, applying, and interpreting that go beyond the obvious and the literal. They are informed by interdisciplinary connections, extrapolation, metaphor, inference, and perspective.

Whole-part-whole: Whole-part-whole is a brain-compatible perspective on learning which suggests that we go from the generality to the specifics and then back to the generality.

Reflection

Working in pairs or trios, establish categories for the terms of differentiation listed below. Give each category a heading.

This workshop serves two purpose. The first is to orient you to the language of differentiated instruction. The second is to demonstrate the process of classification.

Terms

- Academic literacy
- Adjusted questioning
- Alternative assessments (aka authentic assessments, performance tasks)
- Anchor activities
- Bloom's taxonomy (often referred to as "Bloom")
- Brain-based learning
- Choice boards
- Chunking of information
- Clustering
- Compacting
- Constructivism
- Content, process, product
- Cultural capital
- Curriculum components
- Deductive reasoning
- Depth and complexity
- Dialectical journal
- Emotional intelligence
- Embedded application
- Entry points
- Features of differentiation
- Flexible grouping
- Graphic organizer
- Inclusion classes
- Inductive reasoning
- Inquiry activities
- KWL chart
- Learning centers
- Learning contracts
- Learning logs
- Learning profiles
- Learning style
- Microskills and macroskills
- Multiple intelligence theory
- Orbitals
- Portfolios
- Problem-based learning
- Scaffolding
- Schema
- Semantic maps
- "Show what you know" assessments
- Socratic seminar
- Textual features
- Tiered assignments
- Think-pair-share
- Tiered assignments
- Transcendent thinking modes
- Whole-part-whole

4

Language Arts:
Differentiated Instruction for Reading, Vocabulary, Spelling, and Penmanship

A Model for Independent Reading

An effective literacy promotion program includes free choice reading. Research tells us that when it comes to improving reading fluency, stamina, speed, and comprehension, *quantity counts.*

In her second year as principal at McCleary Elementary School, Meg Whitman set the goal of improving reading performance. She wanted to see students doing more reading on their own, and she wanted them to know more about how to read academic information that would help them study and retain.

Meg envisioned her success:

- Students would show an active interest in books: They would purchase their own books, exchange books with others, talk about books, read for pleasure. Anyone walking into McCleary would be able to feel, see, and hear reading in the air.

- Students would show behaviors of purposeful reading of informational text. They would know how to skim, scan, peruse, take notes, review.

- Students would have a variety of reading strategies. They would improve their reading fluency, stamina, patience, and comprehension. What's more, they would understand themselves as readers, knowing how to adjust their reading rates and when to reread.

- Students would have a better vocabulary and sense of written language, which would make them better writers.

Meg needed funding for new and used paperbacks and magazines, classroom bookshelves, a top-notch consultant, and released time for teachers. She knew that although everyone gives lip service to the importance of reading, making actual changes in the school is another story. Changes always cost money and are always to some degree suspect: How do we know that this will work? Meg knew that she'd need research to support her theory, as well as quantitative and qualitative evidence that her ideas about reading had worked to improve student performance.

Meg decided to call her vision *Rx: Reading*. This name was inspired by the American Bookseller's Association's "Prescription for Reading," a program that uses children's visits to their pediatrician's office to encourage reading at an early age. Meg believed that giving her plan a catchy name would unify its components and facilitate publicity. She hoped that the publicity might generate funding and enthusiasm.

After nosing around some sources of research on the long-term benefits of reading for pleasure, Meg decided to rely on two main sources: NCTE's *Reading for Understanding* (Schoenback, Greenleaf, Cziko, and Hurwitz, 1999) and the American Booksellers Association's "Get Caught Reading" website (www.bookweb.org).

Armed with a name, clear goals, and two frameworks (the book and the website), Meg put the call out for a task force. She roped in two of her best language arts teachers, a parent who was active in the parent organization, and a BOE member.

Meg and her task force established the components of *Rx: Reading:*

- **Preassessment:** The preassessment consisted of three parts: a standardized reading test (Degrees of Reading Power), a standardized vocabulary test, and a survey about reading behaviors. The survey asked these questions:
  - How much time do you spend per week reading on your own?
  - How much time do you spend per week reading for schoolwork?
  - Do you have reading material for your own enjoyment in your room at home?
  - The last time that you took a long trip or had to wait for a long time outside of home, did you read to pass the time?
  - Have you recommended any reading material to your friends in the last month?

- **SSR (sustained silent reading) time:** The task force wanted to habituate and ritualize reading for pleasure on a daily basis. Beginning modestly, Meg adjusted the schedule to allow for 10 to 20 minutes once a week, working up to 10 to 20 minutes of pleasure reading per day. These set-aside times for reading in some schools are called "DEAR," an acronym for "Drop Everything And Read."

  Meg ran into a few objections to the SSR time: Some teachers were nervous because of the nature of the reading material that students brought in. "What if a parent objects that the kid is reading a book with objectionable material?" Still others objected to the material themselves, insisting that kids shouldn't be allowed to read "trash" in school. They wanted to have kids do assigned reading during SSR, reading that related to their current topics. Because this was a matter of academic freedom, Meg couldn't impose the "read whatever you want" philosophy on teachers. She knew, going into *Rx:Reading,* that it wouldn't work in all classrooms. She persevered without pushing. Meg kept the faith that, eventually, reading would sell itself.

- **Book ownership and availability:** The task force came up with several ways to get more books into the hands of more kids:
  - They made it possible for kids to exchange books by collecting paperbacks in the library.
  - They provided as many classes as possible with small bookshelves filled with paperbacks and magazines for SSR.
  - They arranged to take students to a local bookstore and give them a book allowance. Meg thought the purpose of this would be obvious: to familiarize kids with the culture of a good bookstore, to encourage them to visit bookstores in their leisure time, to spark book-talking among peers. The task force was unpleasantly surprised by the negative comments of many teachers who considered the bookstore outing to be a frivolous "shopping trip." Some teachers, administrators, and board members remarked that students had plenty of discretionary income. Why hand them money to purchase books? These kids weren't poor.
  - They supplied all offices with reading material.
- **Modeling:**
  - Meg knew that it was essential for teachers to model reading behaviors during SSR. She didn't want teachers using the time to grade papers or do classroom chores while the kids were reading. She wanted them to read something of their choice in front of the kids. Meg modeled this behavior herself, welcoming the chance to read during the day. She always had her current book out on her desk for kids to see when they were in her office.
  - Meg arranged for teachers to receive in-service credit for participation in literary discussion groups. Each group met for 15 hours (three-hour sessions for five weeks) after school at the public library. The 15 hours consisted of two segments. The fiction segment was divided into Y.A. and children's literature. The nonfiction segment was divided into general nonfiction and books related to social issues in education. The manager of the local bookstore, delighted with *Rx: Reading,* even offered a discount on the books for the in-service teachers.
  - *Rx:Reading* set up a bulletin board outside the gym. Posted on the board were photographs of adults and children in the school reading and comments about books and book recommendations.

- **Training:** Using released time out of class, teachers had three sessions with a top-notch consultant in the field of reading education. The consultant guided teachers through the "Reading Apprenticeship Program" described in *Reading for Understanding*. Briefly, this book shows teachers and administrators how to make kids better subject area readers.
- **Sharing success:** Meg made time at every faculty meeting for teachers to share their successes with *Rx: Reading*. These were *very brief reports*, not opportunities to complain or look for training. Meg saw to it that every teacher received a written summary of the success stories.
- **Posttest and evaluation**

Reflection

1. Discuss what you think would be some of Meg's problems in reaching her goals. How would *Rx: Reading* work in your school? Would all or part of it be worth trying?
2. Discuss how *Rx: Reading* is differentiated instruction.
3. How well did Meg use the four principles given in the beginning of this chapter?

Ten Effective School-Wide Reading Initiatives: An Administrator's Guide

1. Make it possible for children to own books. Book ownership makes a big difference in how kids feel about reading. Have book clubs and book exchanges. Get grants to put money in kids' pockets for a shopping spree at a well-stocked bookstore.

2. Show kids that the adults in their school value reading. If you have your nose in a book when the class files in, someone is bound to ask you what you are reading. Take it from there.

3. Ritualize reading. Set aside time for school-wide SSR or DEAR. Another effective program is "Get Caught Reading," sponsored by the American Association of Publishers.

4. Read aloud to children. They need to hear the dialect and rhythm of literature.

5. Use every possible media opportunity to promote reading. Make book reviews a part of morning announcements, bulletin board displays in the halls, newsletters and school newspapers. Get your local newspaper to run a column of book reviews written by students.

6. Institutionalize reading conversation. Use small group conversation as an alternative assessment to the written book report or book test.

7. Keep plenty of high-interest reading materials around. Do whatever you can to bring children together with the kinds of materials they'd like to read.

8. Have the older children read to the little children.

9. Keep teachers up-to-date in the research on the cognitive, social, and emotional dimensions of reading. Employ teachers who believe in a multifaceted, flexible approach to reading instruction. Avoid fads, fanatics, and purists.

10. Encourage teachers to read and share what they've read, including both professional and leisure reading.

Neuroscientists and neurolinguists such as Stephen Pinker tell us that whereas language is instinctive, reading is not. Reading is learned. It comes from the language center of the brain, but there is no "reading center" per se in the brain. The richer the person's language, the more possible it will be to learn to read and to want to read.

Differentiated Instruction Performance Tasks for Reading Assessment

Here are directions to the students for performance tasks. These tasks can be used as formative or summative assessments for independent reading.

The Book Box

The book box is a shoebox in which the student places various items that represent key objects in the story. The student's presentation consists of explaining the significance of these items. This differs from a plot summary in that we are not asking the students to simply retell the story. Rather, we are asking them to identify objects and show how these objects reveal the theme, characterization, setting, and other literary elements. Students usually want to decorate the box in accordance with the story. Advise students that the book box is a collection of loose objects, not a diorama.

The Pitch

You have five minutes with an influential Hollywood producer to pitch your idea for a movie based on this book. Sell it. Go.

Lists and Maps

- ♦ **Props:** List and explain the significance of ten handheld items that appear in the book.
- ♦ **Character star chart:** Express the main and minor characters and their relationships to each other in the form of a chart.
- ♦ **Key verbs:** List and explain 10 key actions in the story. To do this, write 10 key verbs (no synonyms), and explain who does each verb: to whom, when, where, and why.
- ♦ **Obstacle course:** Draw an obstacle course that represents the journey of the main character.

Displays

- ♦ **First and last sentence:** Make an attractive and careful poster using visual images to show the story. Feature the first and the last sentence of the book. Your poster should convey a sense of the atmosphere, setting, key events, and characters.
- ♦ **Multiperceptions:** Make a display that shows how a character feels about herself, how others feel about her, and how the reader feels about her. Refer to specific examples.
- ♦ **Museum exhibit:** Make a model of a museum exhibit that would represent this book in the Literary Museum.

Journals

- ♦ **Double-sided journal:** On the left side, write the literal events. On the right side, write your interpretations, predictions, questions, reactions, theories. This is also called a *dialectical* journal.

Reading Informational Text

The skills involved in reading for information differ from those involved in reading a story. We will refer to these two realms of reading as *informational* and *literary.* Most of our formal reading instruction is on the literary playing field. We then assume, when we transition into informational reading, that the skills are the same. Well, they're not. Here's why:

Literary text invites the reader to linger in the language. When you read a story or a poem, you are expected to read sequentially and to read the whole thing. You follow a story arc, in which you hook onto a character who dwells in a certain (usually well-described) place and follow him or her through the travails of achieving a certain goal—even as that goal is thwarted, advances are made, the character spins around in an ironic twist, and all is resolved one way or the other at the end. The character may speak in a charming voice, the narrator may engage you, there may be side trips and subplots to entertain you. The strategy that you need for literary text is to surrender yourself to the story, envisioning the action within the setting: Put yourself inside the story, stop and smell the roses of the language, expect the unexpected, expect to be entertained.

Although some of those strategies do apply to informational text, reading for information is a different game. Here, we should overview the information first, laying down prior knowledge. We survey the chapter, or the website, or the pamphlet, or the fact sheet before diving into the details. Many readers feel that they are doing something wrong by not reading every word in sequence. But, with informational text, our reading is more purposeful. It's the difference between going into a museum to pass the hours nourishing one's mind and heart and going into the supermarket with a list and in search of certain items. The supermarket shopper is at a great advantage if she knows the layout of the store, what items are likely to be shelved where.

With informational text, as with literary text, learning must be actively constructed (by the learner, with the assistance of the teacher). Some ways of making that happen in differentiated ways are:

- Concept mapping
- Having students make up mock tests
- Summoning prior knowledge
- Using multisensory techniques
- Sharing knowledge and questions with peers

Most informational text is rich with pictures and graphic information. Readers need to learn to integrate multiple forms of information. Some differentiated ways to do this are as follows:

- Go from word to picture or from picture to word, depending on which is more effective for the individual.
- Develop a strategy for moving around the page.
- Overview captions and headings.

Whole Class Instruction for Informational Text

Some people can envision differentiated instruction only as a divided class in which kids are engaged in different activities, but differentiation occurs during whole class instruction when the teacher's presentation takes learning styles into account. Here is how one teacher's habits of mind as a teacher manifest in whole class instruction that takes individual needs into account:

Theory: *New information must be attached to old information.*

> Action: The teacher is constantly asking, "What does this remind you of? Where have you seen this before?" This habit of mind trains students to think of ways of accessing new information.

Theory: *Students need to personalize the information.*

> Action: In a science lesson, the teacher gets students in the habit of mind of personalizing new information by asking, "Have you ever seen this? Felt this? How do you think it would feel at the equator? What would it look like? Sound like? Smell like?"

Theory: *Learning is best when it is multisensory.*

> Action: By definition, informational text is detailed and statistical. It helps to use color coding, to encourage student talk, to provide visuals, to teach note-taking skills.

Theory: *Learners are most effective when they recognize patterns.*

Action: Informational text is presented in a pattern: cause/effect paragraphs, descriptions, chronologies, reasons and examples, comparison/contrast.

Theory: *Metaphor is a powerful learning tool.*

Action: How are the clouds like the currents of the sea? How are they different?

Theory: *Humor is a powerful learning tool.*

Action: Although meteorology may not seem like the most amusing subject in the world, weather reports are one of the most lampoon-able genres because of their familiarity and serious tone. There's always someone in the class who would be happy to play weatherman.

Differentiating Content, Process, and Product in the Textbook

Differentiating Content

Do students need to learn all of the information in the chapter? If they do, then we don't want to differentiate content. But before we make that blanket statement, let's consider the alternatives. Perhaps we want students to learn a few key concepts and a given list of terms. Perhaps we want their learning to be deeper and more complex on a few concepts in a chapter.

How to Read a Chapter in the Science or Social Studies Textbook

Step 1: Get a partner.

Step 2: By yourself. Read the title, the introduction, and the conclusion.

Step 3: By yourself. Read the title, the introduction again, and all the headings, and look at the pictures. Read the captions of the pictures. Read the diagrams and charts and their titles. Read all the specialized words (boldfaced or italicized). Read the questions at the end of the chapter.

Close your book.

Step 4: With your partner. Put your ideas together to talk about what this chapter is about. You and your partner will share what you already know about this topic.

Step 5: With your partner. Make a mind-map of what you remember about the chapter. Leave plenty of room for details. You and your partner should now come up with a few mental questions that you expect the chapter to answer.

Now, open the book again.

Step 6: By yourself. Now, go ahead and read the chapter.

Step 7: With your partner. Go back to your mind-map and fill in any details that you think are important.

Step 8: By yourself. Reread any parts that you didn't understand.

Guiding Principles for Multisensory Reading Programs

To teach all children to read, you need to have as many strategies in your bag of tricks as possible. No one method will work for all children. The progenitor of many successful reading instruction paradigms is the "Orton-Gillingham-Stulman Approach." There are other paradigms that are offshoots of O-G. Although each of these paradigms takes serious, long-term professional training, we present a few of the most tried-and-true ones here as a starter kit.

- ◆ **Orton-Gillingham-Stulman:** This is a highly structured, well-packaged, widely available program stressing learning through the senses. Their slogan is "seeing, hearing, and feeling the difference." O-G is a balanced literacy approach, meaning that it combines phonics with real text experiences (part-to-whole). Reading, writing, and spelling skills are integrated and embedded into all subject areas. A variant of O-G, which includes cursive handwriting and dictionary skills, is MTA (Multisensory Teaching Approach), developed by Margaret Taylor Smith.

- ◆ Other reading programs that are offshoots of O-G:
  - ◆ **The Herman Method:** This remedial reading curriculum teaches decoding, sight words, structural analysis, contextual clues, and dictionary skills. The Herman Method is specifically designed for students with dyslexia/specific reading disability.
  - ◆ **Project READ:** Project READ is a basal reading system involving direct instruction with an emphasis on multisensory input. Targeted for students with delayed reading skills, it stresses concrete inductive instruction.
  - ◆ **Wilson Reading System:** Targeted for children with language-based learning disabilities, the Wilson System is a 12-step remedial program for reading and writing. It emphasizes decoding, phonics, and spelling. It includes components for expressive language and comprehension through visualizing.
  - ◆ **Lindamood-Bell:** This is an intensive treatment for reading, spelling, language comprehension, visual motor processing, and ability to follow oral directions.
  - ◆ **Slingerland:** All learning is through auditory, visual, and tactile motor channels, emphasizing the linking of these channels for those with dyslexia. Beginning with the single letter, the

Slingerland approach reinforces connections to inner-sensory associations.

Vocabulary

Consider the role of learning new words throughout the day. How many new words will your students encounter in a given day? Week? Month? What are the built-in systems of reinforcing these new words? How are the words repeated, rehearsed, and revisited? What opportunities do you provide for students to manipulate and use these new words? What are the relationships between and overlaps from one subject to another? How can students learn to use the same word in different contexts?

The achievement gap is a language gap. The language gap is a vocabulary gap. This section shows you how to differentiate instruction in vocabulary based on sound pedagogy. We learn vocabulary most effectively when:

- New words are repeated, rehearsed, reviewed, revisited.
- New words are presented in meaningful contexts.
- New words are modeled enthusiastically.
- New words are used in various forms.
- New words are connected to word families.

Traditional Vocabulary Teaching: Language Arts

For years, Ms. Evans taught vocabulary using a workbook. The workbook was divided into chapters and units, each chapter presenting a list of 25 unrelated words and definitions. On Monday, Ms. Evans pronounced the words for the students and had them read the definitions aloud. Monday, Tuesday, and Wednesday night's homework was to fill in the exercises in the workbook: sentence blanks, matching, word finds, jumbles. Every day she would review the homework. On Friday there would be a test on the week's words; every few weeks there would be a cumulative test.

Mrs. Bloom used vocabulary taken from readings. She would write a list of words on the board that students would meet in their assigned reading. Students were required to write dictionary definitions of these words, compose original sentences, and know the words for the unit test on the assigned reading.

These two teachers found no surprises in their students' performance on their vocabulary tests: Good students usually did well; weak students usually did poorly. One thing was certain: No one was really improving their vocabulary in speech or writing because there was little to no crossover between the words the students studied and the words they used.

After some training in differentiating instruction, Ms. Evans and Mrs. Bloom improved their vocabulary instruction. That is, their students began showing an interest in the words, using them in speech and writing, and remembering them.

Ms. Evans wanted to hold on to her vocabulary workbook. She liked the built-in reinforcement and homework. She knew that students would have to spend more time with the words, but she couldn't spare more class time and didn't want more paperwork for herself. Mrs. Bloom wanted to continue to use words encountered in the basal reader. Like Ms. Evans, she didn't want to devote more class time to vocabulary instruction. Here is how Ms. Evans and Mrs. Bloom used the pedagogy of differentiated instruction to make vocabulary instruction more robust and durable:

- *Less is more.* Ms. Evans asked students to pick out 10 of the 25 words in each chapter to learn for the week. She suggested that they select words that they had heard of but had never actually used. Mrs. Bloom asked students to scan the basal reader on the lookout for 10 "interesting" words. Students then used sticky flags to mark these words.

- *Context.* A dictionary or glossary definition is bloodless. A word has to breathe, stretch, jump around in real time. Ms. Evans and Mrs. Bloom made a conscious effort to teach vocabulary just by using the words themselves and encouraging kids to use them. They reminded kids whenever a "word opportunity" came up in their speech. Those words were written on the board, just waiting to be pressed into service. Doing this, they used the words metaphorically, in various grammatical situations, in various forms. They also asked for "word sightings," times in which "our words" were heard in other classes, on television, in the movies.

- *Visuals.* Instead of doing matching columns, Ms. Evans began asking her students to draw pictures in their notebooks to represent the words, especially the nouns. She would spend just a few minutes at the start of class having students draw their diagrams on the board or post them in the vocabulary center.

- *Vocabulary center.* In a prominent place in the classroom, Ms. Evans and Mrs. Bloom set up posters, visuals, model sentences, and other displays to remind students of their words.

- *Personalizing.* Ms. Evans and Mrs. Bloom asked students to write brief statements about their own lives, incorporating the new words.

- *Storytelling.* Ms. Evans and Mrs. Bloom had students retell familiar stories and fairy tales, using the words that they were learning.

Levels of word-knowing:

1. I use this word in my speech and writing.
2. I know what this word means, but I've never used it myself.

3a. I've heard of this word, I have some idea what it means, and I'm interested in it.

3b. I've heard of this word, I have some idea what it means, but I'm not interested in it.

4a. I've never heard of this word, but I'm interested in it.

4b. I've never heard of this word, and I'm not interested in it.

Three Ways to Learn New Words

The work of Allan Hunt and David Beglar divides vocabulary learning into three categories:

♦ **Incidental learning:** Incidental learning of new words happens when students are exposed to extensive reading and are listening to language at their instructional level. Teachers can support incidental learning by making it a habit to elevate their own language level, defining words in context, when speaking to students.

♦ **Explicit instruction:** Explicit instruction happens when teachers present and analyze new words for students, helping them to understand structure, suffixes, and prefixes. Explicit instruction involves expanding on a dictionary definition by assisting students with using the word in context in its different forms, providing practice in usage and pronunciation, and building a learning environment in which new words are nurtured.

♦ **Independent strategy development:** Independent strategy development should be the goal of explicit instruction, in which students learn how to learn new words through contextual clues, dictionary and glossary use, etymology, and maximizing personal learning style such as visualization, memorization, categorization.

Effective vocabulary instruction for native speakers involves the interweaving of these three pathways. This means that teachers exploit teachable moments to teach word roots, synonyms, antonyms, and nuances as new words appear in context. Many teachers do this by reading aloud, stopping along the way to teach what is likely to be a new word to most students. Although students are probably using an age-appropriate dictionary in your class, they may be using a collegiate dictionary at home. Such dictionaries are less than effective for elementary schoolchildren. You might make some suggestions to the parents accordingly.

Teach not only single words, but expressions, phrases, figures of speech, and metaphor.

Here are some adaptations of the principles of word-learning proposed by Hunt and Beglar:

♦ *Incidental learning of new words is all about exposure.* Read, read, read. The more students read, no matter *what* they read, the more they are building stamina and fluency. Even if they choose to read low-level materials, they are still incidentally learning much about language structure, spelling, syntax, suffixes, prefixes, and word roots.

♦ *Concentrate on high-frequency words.* When giving explicit instruction, use your common sense and word experience to prioritize words. What words are students most likely to use, hear, and read? Remember that even though students may be able to deliver a dictionary definition of a word, they may not tend to use that word in their own vocabulary. Such words are worthy of explicit instruction, because the idea is to expand the students' actual deployment of more words.

♦ *Nurture new words.* We need to provide opportunities and reminders for students to use new words purposefully. While incidental (contextual) learning is the most natural and effective way to learn new words, we can expand our students' word knowledge by explicit instruction. Explicit word-teaching is most effective when the word is used in meaningful contexts; it is least effective when words are isolated, such as in a matching column. Giving students isolated words does not how them how to fit the word grammatically into a sentence, how to change its form, how its meaning is shaded.

If you are using a list, ask students to make cards for each word. That way, they can arrange the cards in an order that best suits their needs. The process of sorting and categorizing is itself instructional. To differentiate instruction, students can add information to the cards, such as synonyms, antonyms, etymological information, related words, mnemonic devices.

The paradox of word-learning is that the best way to improve vocabulary is by exposure to reading and listening, but the learner needs a certain level of language in order to understand what she's reading or hearing in the first place. Thus, we need to supplement incidental learning with explicit teaching. This paradox is especially applicable to English language learners.

♦ *Be deliberate in how you cluster words.* Learning one word provides an opportunity to learn its family and friends. Present words in clusters based on semantics (synonyms, antonyms), etymology (prefixes, suffixes, roots). If words are similar in form but semantically unrelated, it can be confusing to learn them together. This is the danger of teaching words alphabetically: Just because words look alike doesn't mean that they are semantically similar, although very often there is a relation between look-alike words.

♦ *It's better to learn a few words thoroughly over time than to try to learn many words over a short spurt of time.* The largest window of forgetting happens just after new information is learned. Deeper mental processing and retention are more likely to take place if you practice repetition and review of fewer words. Try teaching 5 to 7 words per week rather than 20 to 30. To get more mileage out of the 5 to 7 words, teach them along with related words.

♦ *Provide opportunities for elaborating on word knowledge.* Knowing a word means a great deal more than just being able to recite its dictionary definition. To know a word, you have to know its guides: How can it be adapted to fit different grammatical forms? What affixes does it take? You have to know its neighborhood, where it hangs out: What are its connotations? Associations? Nuances? We speak of receptive knowledge, or being able to recognize the word when it is used by others, and productive knowledge, or using the word in one's own speech and writing. The latter requires a deeper understanding and more practice than the former. Teaching a word for deep understanding means providing opportunities for practice, placing the word in original contexts, using the word both literally and figuratively. Is this a word that is likely to be found in ordinary speech, or is it a technical term? Does this word carry emotional baggage, or is it neutral? How fixed or flexible is its definition?

♦ *Work toward fluency.* To work toward fluency with new words, we need to integrate the new with the known vocabulary. Where will the new words find a place in a student's own language? Conversational practice is essential. Here again, extensive reading and listening to elevated vocabulary in meaningful contexts work to develop fluency. Fluent readers don't read individual words, but groups of words, a habit that can be learned and practiced. One effective way to improve reading fluency is timed readings, in which readers practice timed reading on passages that they have already read, increasing their speed with each reading and monitoring their reading techniques as they do so.

♦ *Learning to guess.* Strategic guessing at the meaning of unfamiliar words is an independent reading strategy. However, to guess from context, the learner has to already know 95% of the words. We can't expect a student who is reading above her head to be very good at guessing through context.. Guessing from context is more effective for the high-level student, and this is something to remember as we differentiate vocabulary instruction.

There is a procedure for guessing from context: First, decide whether the word is important enough to learn: Is it repeated? Does it seem essential to meaning? This decision itself is a reading skill. Next determine the function of the word in the sentence:

What is its grammatical job? Simplify the sentence by bracketing unnecessary words. Then examine the immediate vicinity of the word. At this point, make an educated guess as to the meaning of the word, and check with a dictionary, glossary, or, better yet, the teacher. Be sure that the guess is in the same part of speech as the target word. Use affixes as clues. This strategy is best when used instructionally, demonstrated by the teacher. Teachers provide richer and more memorable definitions than dictionaries.

♦ *Learning about formal and informal speech.* Every year of their schooling, children have to discern when it is appropriate to use informal or slang speech (in conversations with their friends, at home) and when they need to shift gears into formal (school) speech. Informal speech is not incorrect if it suits its audience and purpose. Neither is formal speech the correct choice for every speech occasion. Use dialects found in literature to point out this distinction. Have children role play different speech environments calling for formal or informal language.

Teachers need to plan a wide array of activities, exercises, conversational contexts, and reinforcements in order to effectively teach students to learn new words. The instructional plan must embrace incidental learning, explicit instruction, and independent learning strategies. Vocabulary learning must be contextual, enthusiastic, purposeful, and gradual if it is to be lasting. Students need to read and listen extensively, elaborate, connect, guess from context, use dictionaries efficiently and thoroughly, use and have students make word walls. Be as lavish as possible with opportunities to use new words.

Assessment: Beyond the Vocabulary Quiz

Ben Trellis gives every student in his language arts classes his or her *own* vocabulary quiz, based on the words each child has decided to learn. Does he go home and make up 112 different quizzes? No. All he does is give the kids a sheet that has 10 blank spaces on the left-hand side, with 10 blank spaces corresponding on the right-hand side. The day before the quiz, Ben's students write down the words that they want to be quizzed on. They write these words down the left-hand column. They've taken these words from their readings in the basal reader or from the newspaper. The next day, he hands them back their own quizzes and has them fill in definitions in the right-hand column.

Ben's students keep a vocabulary journal. They select a certain number of words per week. Each word is written in the center of their journal page. The page is then filled in with definitions, related words, roots and affixes, other forms of the word, original sentences and phrases, synonyms, and antonyms.

Exploiting Context

Ms. Fiori's way of teaching vocabulary is to make the most of what students already know, using the book, *A Way with Words* (Benjamin, 200a). Here is a sample from this book:

The Emperor's New Vestments

Words You Will Meet:

dominating	regal
conceited	symbolic
urgent	mundane
scarcely	

Paragraph 1:

> Once upon a time, there lived a *dominating* and *regal* Emperor who had a *conceited* streak a mile wide. He was so interested in *symbolic* clothing that he *scarcely* had time to tend to the *urgent* needs of running a kingdom.

Practice
Picture the Words

Draw a picture of:

Conceited Clementine	Dave the Despot
Edgar the Egotist	Vincent the Vestment Vendor

Other Word-Learning Performance Tasks

The three tasks presented here work well to advance learning for gifted and talented students, and can be tiered for students at lower levels.

Building a Glossary

Mr. Artiss has students build a glossary in their notebooks. Students are given a list of 100 words from which they are to select 20 every nine weeks. Mr. Artiss suggests that they select words that they have heard of, but are not certain of the meanings. To further differentiate, he uses three lists in increasing order of sophistication. Mr. Artiss has arranged these three lists so that they don't appear obviously leveled: The "easiest" list doesn't necessarily contain short words; nor does the most sophisticated list contain polysyllabic words.

In their glossaries, students must do four things with each word: *define, describe, explain, exemplify, expand.*

- *Define:* Write a dictionary definition in your own words.
- *Describe:* Use words that give a visual image that helps you understand the word.
- *Explain:* Use words that give more information about how this word is used.
- *Exemplify:* Use the word in a meaningful sentence that clearly expresses its meaning.
- *Expand:* Give several forms of this word.

Juicy Sentences

A juicy sentence tells a story. Your juicy sentence must use a word that you've chosen to learn in a sentence that tells: Who? What? Why? When? and How?

Clustering

Clustering is a technique in which you consider how words are alike and how they are different. From the word list, form several categories, each consisting of at least five words. Use your imagination to form the categories: connotation (positive, negative, neutral), parts of speech, structure, visuals/nonvisuals. Not all of the words in the group have to fit into your categories. Feel free to change the form of the words. You may have a few leftovers.

Spelling

Spelling comes into the conversation about vocabulary for two reasons: The spelling of a word gives us clues to its meaning, and we are more likely to use a word in writing if we are confident about its spelling.

Spelling is one of the most teachable skills and one of the easiest to differentiate instruction for. Mirroring its diverse speakers, English is a complex, amalgamated language. It is much more systematic and predictable than we give it credit for. I'll address two myths of spelling instruction: that English is a crazy language and that you can't teach a bad speller.

The following are various ways to improve spelling:

- *Explanations:* "I need to know why." Contrary to popular belief, the English language is largely sensible if you know how to group words. People who learn by intellectualizing should learn the rules of dropping and doubling letters. They should also learn patterns and groupings, for example, that *ght* words are Anglo-Saxon in derivation, while words with a *y* as the second letter are Greek. Teach gifted and talented students how to use the etymological information in the dictionary to understand more about the *why* of spelling. Think of words as the archeologist would: A word's history gives clues to its construction. Prefixes are simply tacked on to the beginning of a word, while suffixes are added in accordance with certain fairly reliable rules.

- *Repetition:* "I need to go over and over it." Learners with a strong musical sense can learn to spell through finding the rhythm of the words. This involves spelling the words out loud, in groups, tapping out the rhythm. Mnemonics often rely on rhythm, such as "Climb the ladder of success: s-u-c-c-e-s-s."

- *Kinesthetics:* "I need to know it in my hands." "Air writing" works well for many learners. Many people can't spell in their heads. They need to actually write the word, either on paper or in the air. Perhaps this is a combination of the kinesthetic and the visual.

- *Visuals:* "I need to see it." Most people are strong visual learners. Posting words around the room is a powerful reinforcer. Some people visually exaggerate the danger zone of the word.

- *Multisensory combinations:* "I need the whole body spelling experience." The see-say-write method has proven useful for special education students.

Gifted and talented students are adept at finding patterns and reasons for the rules and exceptions of English spelling. For example, words that are exceptions to the "I before E except after C rule" can be transformed into a -*ception* form: *conceive/conception; receive, reception; deceive/deception.* This connection makes sense out of spelling for students who have advanced verbal skills

Learning to spell is all about metacognition: learning how to learn. Effective lessons are ongoing, integrated, exploitative of the teachable moment, and enthusiastic. But whatever you do to teach spelling, please don't ever present the misspelled word next to the correct word and ask the student which one is correct. What that does is to reinforce the negative, tricking the brain into thinking that wrong is right. Never take the chance that the learner's brain won't decide to latch on to the misspelled word, taking the incorrect mental snapshot.

Reflection

1. What can students learn about words from the dictionary? What are the limitations of using the dictionary to teach vocabulary?

2. Explain how and why any of the ideas in this section will change the way students learn new words in your class.

3. Add other strategies for differentiating vocabulary instruction.

4. How could you use the following manipulatives to stimulate interest in word-learning?

- ice-cream sticks
- a beach ball with Velcro strips
- a deck of cards
- construction paper
- colored markers
- small assignment pads
- index cards

Differentiated Instruction for Penmanship

In this digital age, concern about penmanship may seem quaint at best, outdated at worst. However, we can't deny that children still need to write legibly, preferably in both print and cursive, capitals and lower-case. In elementary and secondary schools, there are still many situations, notably in-class exams requiring essays or full-sentence response, for which legible communication is essential. The student whose penmanship makes the reading task difficult for the teacher is disadvantaged: No one looks kindly upon written material that mystifies the naked eye. We want, have a right to have, the reader's message accessible.

In teaching penmanship, we run into a conflict of interest: On the one hand (literally), we think of penmanship as highly idiosyncratic—stylized for the individual's own personal flair. The very word "signature" evokes uniqueness. However, some writing is so unique that it is pretty much impossible for anyone other than the one person who wrote it to read it. OK, that's *too* stylized! Whatever our philosophy, whether we think penmanship should be taught by the famous Palmer method, or whether we think the page is the place to practice rugged individualism, we can all agree on one thing about legibility: Letters are supposed to identify themselves clearly, and at first glance.

Handwriting, being a physical skill, is developed and ingrained through habit. It operates by muscle memory. Practice makes permanent. As with all muscular skills, whether it be playing the piano or throwing a ball, unlearning bad habits is very difficult—hence the importance of careful early training.

There's an emotional and social element at work here, and you overlook it at your own peril. *Suffice it to say this: I need to read your handwriting. For me to do that, you need to make your letters identify themselves.*

Speed, bad habits, excessive ornateness for stylistic effect, lack of explicit instruction and sufficient practice, the desire to mask spelling errors, rebellion and defiance (this, more in the upper grades): These are some of the nonphysical reasons for illegible handwriting, some of which can be overcome by the simple demand that written work be legible when it is handed in. But we should probably avoid condemnatory adjectives when talking to children about their handwriting. Labels such as "sloppy," "a mess," and "careless" are not the most productive ways of bringing out the best in children.

I do not mean to be cavalier about students with fine motor skills deficits, students with tremors, muscular weaknesses, emotional problems about writing, or other disabilities. I spent my elementary years feeling shame about my "sloppy" handwriting, and the telltale ink stains on the side of my left hand, not to mention the smudges on the paper from dragging my left hand across it. (This doesn't happen when one writes in Hebrew, a more left-friendly language.) My point is that, leaving aside for the moment that fine handwriting is unattainable for certain children, differentiated instruction can be well used to teach penmanship.

First, the diagnosis. Here are seven points at which communication breaks down between the writer and the reader, resulting in the reader not being able to read a certain word at first glance:

- *The breakdown of letter-size differentiation:* Many writers get into the habit of making all letters the same height. When *e*'s are the same height as *l*'s, *h*'s the same height as *n*'s, the reader can't read the word at first glance.

- *The breakdown of spacing between words and letters:* Failure to provide adequate demarcation space between one word and the next is a common flaw, simple to fix because it is a matter of habit. Ideally, letters should be equidistant, but we'll settle for just being able to see where one word and letter begins and ends. Often the problem is with extended loops at the ends of words, where the writer has failed to lift the pen from the page in going from one word to the next. Graph paper can be helpful.

- *The breakdown of rounding:* When the lower-case *a* looks like a *u*, we have a rounding problem. The famous (and undeservedly outdated)

Palmer method has children making endless coils. These, interspersed with parallel lines, teach the muscles to alternate between circles and lines.

♦ *The breakdown of closing up:* When the *r* and the *s* look the same, when the *c* and the *o* look the same, when the *a* and the *u* look the same, we have a closing-up problem. Again, the circle and line practice can help.

♦ *The breakdown of detail:* Dotting *i*'s (and *j*'s) and crossing *t*'s are metaphors for paying attention to detail. Especially if the writing tends to be loopy, making *e*'s that look like *i*'s, and *l*'s that resemble *t*'s, the jots and tittles, as dots and crosses used to be called, aid in legibility.

♦ *The breakdown of looping:* To loop or not to loop: That is the difference between *l* and *e*. "Little" is a good practice word for this habit.

♦ *The breakdown of elegance:* By *elegance,* we mean the beauty of simplicity. Dotting *i*'s with circles, crossing *t*'s with ostentatious lines across the whole word, superfluous loops, and other embellishments distract from the identity of the letter. These flourishes impede the reader, as she subconsciously discards the wheat from the chaff. I'll also include here the breakdown of elegance that occurs when we see the writer sweat: Excessive pressure on the writing implement should not be apparent. The reader should not feel the writer's pain.

Now the DI prescription: Mrs. Van Buren assigns children to the Penmanship Station to work on specific skills when she notices lapses. In the station, she has various surfaces and writing implements from which the children can choose. They may leave the station when they've shown Mrs. Van Buren that they've copied a piece of American rhetoric to her satisfaction. The choices are: The Gettysburg Address; the "Ask not what your country can do for you . . . " statement from the JFK inaugural; the Pledge of Allegiance; the first sentence of the Declaration of Independence; the words to "The Star-Spangled Banner," "God Bless America," "America the Beautiful," or "This Land Is Your Land." When deemed worthy (fully legible and flawlessly copied), their work gets an American flag sticker and is posted in the Museum of American Letters, a corkboard in the writing station.

The materials in the Penmanship Station are traditional handwriting practice notebooks (the kind with the broken lines), large index cards, flip chart paper, graph paper, dry-erase boards, chalkboards, model alphabets, tracing paper, handwriting workbooks, videos, CD-ROMs, plastic letters, magnetic letters, erasers, paper stabilizers pencil grippers, and all kinds of writing implements.

The Penmanship Station

HERE'S WHERE YOU NEED TO IMPROVE YOUR PENMANSHIP

1. Be careful about letter sizes: _____
   Make sure your short letters are short and your tall letters are tall.

2. Close up your letters: _____

3. Space your words: _____
   There should be a space big enough to fit the letter o between each word.

4. Write a little bigger: _____

5. Don't scrunch: _____

6. Dot and cross: _____

7. Practice circles and lines: _____

8. Simplify! _____

YOUR JOB

1. You received a paper that says P-Station on it. Have that with you at the station.
2. Look at the item(s) checked above.
3. You must do one of the following things to practice:
   A. Rewrite the part of your paper that needs the rule.
   B. Do a practice card for that rule. (Take a practice card from the card rack.)
4. Do a page of circles and lines. Everybody in the P-Station has to do a page of lines and circles every time they visit.
5. When you think you've had enough practice, you may take a Copy Me card and write it as clearly as you can.
6. Show your Copy Me card to Mrs. Van Buren. She will tell you what to do next.

Ms. Colby's Rules: Simplify, Clarify, Intensify

Ms. Colby compacts the handwriting rules into three maxims:

Simplify. Readable handwriting should have no extra lines or loops to distract the reader.

Clarify. Every letter should look exactly like itself, and not like any other letter.

Intensify. Readable penmanship has contrast: contrast of height, contrast of circles and lines, contrast of being closed or open. When we intensify the contrast, we make our letters look more like themselves.

Mr. Miles' "You Gotta BE the Letters"

Mr. Miles tells his students that every letter is proud to be itself. "If I'm a lower-case *a*," he says, "that means I'm rounded out. I'm rounded out, but I'm nice and straight on the right side. And I'm closed up tight on my top."

Mr. Miles has adapted Jeffrey Willheim's theories on reading engagement (*You Gotta BE the Book*, Columbia Teachers College) to penmanship teaching. Each child in his third grade class speaks in the voice of a letter or a word. "It's about the verbs," he explains. "The actions. Writing is action: We're swooping, we're rounding, we're going up, we're coming down. We're staying straight, hanging down, standing tall."

By connecting penmanship to narrative and physicality, Mr. Miles plays into multiple intelligence theory and learning styles. "Penmanship involves not only verbal and kinesthetic skills, but also artistic sensibilities and music. Rhythm. Like any well-controlled, sustained motor activity, penmanship has its rhythm. I use counting exercises to practice the circles and lines, then the letters. We do a lot of air-writing, visualizing, and, of course, repetition.

Mr. Gleason and the Lefties

Left-handers have varying degrees of ambidexterity; some have little difficulty adapting to a right-handed world, but for others, it is a struggle, especially in elementary school.

In days of old, lefties were considered evil, possessed by the devil (that is where the word *sinister* comes from, as does the word *gauche*); lefties were forced to "convert." Today, that would be done only in the most retrograde of schools, and even the classic "lefty slant" is not frowned upon as "wrong," as it was when I went to school.

If you want to know how the world looks to a lefty's eyes, hold a pen that has writing on it in your right hand. You can read the letters. Now, hold that pen in your left hand. You're reading the letters upside down. Watch a lefty take a picture with a camera. She's using her "wrong" hand to click the shutter. She goes to her piano lesson and has a tougher time than her right-handed friends, because the quick-changing keys are played with the right hand, while the chords are played with the left. And we've already talk about the ink-stained hand. Mr. Gleason provides talc! It works!

Lefties tend to hook their hands when they write. They need to tilt the paper to the right. And Mr. Gleason has found that lefty kids take to the keyboard with alacrity, finding relief from the frustrations of learning how to write longhand.

- ♦ **Techniques that improve penmanship.** The following activities build muscle memory and fluidity:
  - ♦ Tracing
  - ♦ Finger painting

- ◆ Constructing letters out of clay; carving letters into clay
- ◆ Air-writing
- ◆ Practicing circles, arcs, and lines
- ◆ Drawing waves on the sea
- ◆ Joining the letters.
  - ◆ Letters that finish at the top join horizontally (*o, r, v, w, t, f*).
  - ◆ Letters that finish at the bottom join diagonally.
  - ◆ Letters that finish on a left-moving stroke are best left unjoined (*b, g, j, p, s, y*).
- ◆ **Advancing levels.** Students with good penmanship skills who are inclined to make them better can learn calligraphy, make greeting cards, make captions for bulletin boards, design class stationery.
- ◆ **Other Handwriting Projects.**
  - ◆ Compare and contrast your handwriting to that of your siblings and parents.
  - ◆ Compare your handwriting now to what it was two grade levels ago.
  - ◆ Learn about other alphabets: Chinese, Hebrew, Cyrillic.
  - ◆ Learn about different writing implements used through history.
- ◆ **Penmanship glossary.**
  - ◆ *calligraphy* (from the root in Latin meaning "beautiful writing")
  - ◆ *ascenders* [letters that have a height reaching to the top of the line (*d, h, l, t*)]
  - ◆ *descenders* [letters that have tails that drop below the line (*f, g, p, y*)]
  - ◆ *equidistant*
  - ◆ *symmetrical*
  - ◆ *parallel*

Occupational Therapy: The Texture Experience

Because you might teach students with sensory integration deficits, O.T. methodology may be helpful. Autistic children often have great difficulties interacting with anything textual or interacting with anything outside the self. Since handwriting is a textual, outside-the-self experience, you may find O.T. a place to begin.

We've already mentioned finger painting. Your students may have success with sand, or other gritty substances (salt) in the finger paint. Use texture cards, made by pieces of cardboard covered with nappy fabric (corduroy, ter-rycloth, velvet, fleece) to have the child match like pairs of textures. You may try "full-handed" textural experiences, such as bags of rice, popcorn, uncooked pasta, plastic beads, cereal. (Of course, special needs children differ widely in what they can reasonably be expected to handle.) With these materials, the child may be up to scooping, pouring, counting, sorting, measuring.

If you dare, add water. Misters (spray bottles, not the aersol type) are the least messy way to use water.

And there's always play dough with its infinite variety of molds in the shapes of letters, numbers, geometrics.

Summary

Language learning is arguably the most important thing we teach, because language is infused in all subjects. To build capacity with language, students must be exposed to as much reading at their comfort level and instructional level as possible. To become better readers, they need explicit and implicit vocabulary instruction. Spelling can be differentiated in the context of vocabulary instruction.

Penmanship is not a critical thinking skill. It's a motor skill, highly dependent on getting the fundamentals right. We should not take for granted that "some people just have chicken scratch for handwriting," and we shouldn't overlook the fact that those people will be disadvantaged later in school when teachers have to read their handwritten essays, which is still a fact of life. Just as children learn to adjust their speech registers depending on audience and purpose, so should they have a "dress-up" handwriting for writing that others will read, and a "dress-down" one suitable for notes and other personal writings.

5

Teaching for Abstract Thinking

In the movie *Billy Madison*, the title character, played by Adam Sandler, has to return to school as an adult and repeat his school years, one week for each grade, to prove to his father that he's worthy to take over the family business. Billy does fine in kindergarten. He sails through his week in first grade, and on to the second. But in just half a minute in the third grade, Billy panics: "Multiplication! This is where it gets really hard." Billy is onto something. Although abstract thinking is more a function of secondary education, along about third grade, we do expect kids to begin breaking away from concrete thinking and toward abstract representational thinking.

Some theory: In their seminal book, *Language in Thought and Action*, S. I. Hayakawa and Alan R. Hayakawa (1965) elaborate on the "ladder of abstraction model" developed by the Polish mathematician Alfred Korzybski. When Korzybski defected to the United States during World War I, he turned his studies to mental health and communications. As a mathematician, he understood well the significance of abstraction. He extrapolated that knowledge to develop a theory of how language works in communication, or how language is misunderstood because communicators don't comprehend the nature of symbolism: *The word is not the thing. The word is the symbol of the thing it represents. If it symbolizes something different for me than it does for you, then our communication misfires.*

Hayakawa built upon this idea. He tells us to remember that "words never say all about anything." The more abstract the word, the more it does not say everything. *Abstract* means "to draw away." As we abstract, we draw certain characteristics away from the thing itself, and we conceptualize what we have drawn away by giving it a name and by grouping it with like things that share the abstraction. The more concrete the word is, the more we can agree, and therefore communicate, about its meaning. We reference the same mental picture for *black cat*. But we don't reference the same mental picture for an abstraction, such as *government*, or *love*, or *power*.

The relevance of these philosophical ideas is that to differentiate instruction, we need to be aware of how our students process concrete language (language that references concrete things) and abstract language (language that references things that we don't all mentally see or experience in the same way). To communicate with our students, we need to understand how they process concrete language. And to elevate their thinking beyond the concrete level, we need to understand how they process abstractions.

Here's how the abstraction ladder works: On the lowest level, we have a specimen, such as Bessie the cow. A higher level of abstraction (but still on the concrete level) is *cow*. If I see a creature who looks a lot like Bessie, I extrapolate, because of what I know about Bessie, that such a creature is called a *cow*. BUT, I am leaving out some of Bessie's characteristics when I call the other "Bessie" a cow. Maybe I'm leaving out the fact that Bessie is white with brown spots, while the generalized *cow* has a different kind of coloration. In going from one level of abstraction to another, I will select particular commonalities and leave out certain differences. And I will continue that thought process up the ladder.

Now, on the third level is the larger generalization that a cow is a member of the group called *livestock.* In naming cows *livestock,* I have a bunch of cows, each sharing key characteristics that I choose to pay attention to. I find other animals—pigs, chickens and turkeys—that live on the farm. I choose to ignore the differences between the cows and the other animals when I call them all *livestock.* I'm abstracting (drawing away) certain characteristics as I go up the ladder, naming things, conceptualizing them.

The fourth level will be *farm assets.* I'll abstract the value of my livestock and put it together with other things on my farm that I can sell for money or that can produce money for me. *Farm assets* are brought to the fifth level: *assets.* These include my farm assets, plus the other salable goods that I own in my personal life or in additional businesses and investments. Note at this point that we still have Bessie in all this, but more and more of her personal (cow-like) characteristics are left out of consideration. The higher up the abstraction ladder I climb, the more selective I am in including the items on the lower, more concrete levels.

The sixth rung in the example, the highest, would be *wealth. Wealth* is more abstract than *asset,* and it is interesting, elevated thinking to consider why. In conceiving of *wealth,* we draw away (abstract) something from *asset.* To see how far we've come on the abstraction ladder, how much we've drawn away and left behind, compare *Bessie* now to *wealth.* That is what abstract thinking does: It selects certain characteristics upon which to make generalities, bringing in more examples that display those characteristics.

As you can see, the abstraction ladder is both mathematical and semantic. It has to do with conceptions and communications, which is why I mentioned that it is the brainchild of a mathematician-turned-communications-specialist, and was then piggybacked upon by a semanticist.

If I were to describe the abstraction ladder to you without giving you the concrete examples, you probably would not understand it. (I know I wouldn't.)

The reason is that we, like our students, need concrete examples to understand abstract concepts. Master teachers know this, as do effective writers. The practical application is that we need to achieve a balance between the concrete and the abstract in our communication. If we disregard the concrete, then we risk not being understood by those who need concrete examples. But if we are *too* concrete, then we fail to convey the overarching truths, generalities, theories.

Let's return to Billy Madison and the third grade. The first thing he may notice about the third grade, the most striking reason why it looms as "hard," is that the language is becoming abstract. Ruby Payne, a specialist in urban education and poverty issues, has a lot to say about abstract representational systems and their significance in the world of school. She notes: "To survive in poverty, one must be very sensory-based and non-verbal. To survive in school, one must be very verbal and abstract" (Payne, 2002, p. 21). Payne gives the example of how a blueprint is the abstract representational system for a house.

Applications to Differentiated Learning

If students have to move from concrete to abstract and back to concrete thinking subconsciously as they proceed through school, it would seem logical to have them develop a conscious awareness of what this means. Below are several thinking exercises that allow students to practice moving up and down the abstraction ladder. They are presented in increasing levels of sophistication.

1. Given two examples, the student names which is more abstract than the other.

2. Given multiple examples, the student orders them from most concrete to most abstract.

3. Students analyze the following statement: *If all generalities are abstractions, are all abstractions generalities?*

4. Have students use the analog clock model to describe where items are located. Thinking of "straight ahead" as 12:00, refer to items being at "1:00," 3:00," 11:00," and so on.

5. Using a map of the United States, or other familiar system, in a fashion similar to that of number 4 above, have students refer to an item as being in "Michigan," or "California."

6. Use the language of orientation in space and time. Practice identifying an item as to where it is in relation to another item using directionality words (*left, right, north, south, east, west, horizontally, vertically*) and space measurement words (*meters, feet, inches, degrees*) and time words (*before, after, yesterday, tomorrow, last year*). Use calendars, planning diaries, and timelines.

7. Use reference tables, keys, and legends to understand symbolic representations such as maps.

8. Teach visual transport. This is the skill of holding a picture in your mind and then mentally superimposing it onto something real (see number 4 above).

9. Teach students to develop a personal system of symbols to use for their homework pads, notes, and personal reminders.

10. Use concept maps.

11. Encourage and model refined vocabulary. Discourage the use of lazy fillers, such as "the whatchamacallit" or "the thingy." These are poor communication habits that miss opportunities to sharpen language.

12. Develop an awareness of semiotics (symbols) all around us: highway signs, signs in the school, signs on television, signs in toys.

13. When teaching writing or oral presentations, encourage the habit of going from general to specific, and back to general.

14. Identify concrete words and abstract words in readings. Note the kinds of readings that rely on concrete words and those that use more abstract terms.

15. Categorize, taxonomize, analyze. Label accordingly.

16. Find generalities in your readings, and make them more concrete.

17. Practice finding commonalities among seemingly unlike things, and vice versa. Doing so is what abstraction is all about, because to make an abstraction, we must (for the purpose of making the abstraction) ignore differences and draw away similarities.

Abstract Representational Systems and the Subject Areas

Inasmuch as words themselves are abstract representations, the language arts are abstract per se. But within that, we navigate the abstraction ladder as we read stories. The storyteller goes up and down the ladder, now referring to objects, now to ideas, now to specifics, now to generalities. The story gives us insight into life and the world; the specific characters and settings help to get us there and hold our interest. The specifics give us something to hold on to, something we can see and understand, on our way to a larger, abstract understanding. Poetry is famous for conveying the abstract in terms of the concrete—hence Robert Frost's well-known statement that poetry speaks of one thing in terms of another.

Obviously, math is all about abstractions and becomes more so with each grade level. Not only are numbers and operational signs symbolic, but also the number themselves will soon be replaced with x and y.

In science, hypotheses are formed based upon observations. The scientist moves up and down the abstraction ladder by continually checking her hypothesis (abstraction) against the observable concrete phenomena. Predictions, as well, are abstractions to be tested against eventualities.

In social studies, the abstractions are the social systems (democracy, socialism, monarchy) as well as the ideals (justice, civil rights). The specifics are the leaders, the events, the court cases. It is through the concrete (acts, bills, laws, edicts, proclamations) that the abstract ideals (prosperity, equality, liberty) are achieved or prevented.

In the arts, principles of aesthetics are grounded in particular creations. The same applies to engineering, where structural soundness is based upon abstract principles.

Social Studies

Here's how Mrs. Francis, third grade teacher, embeds abstract thinking in a differentiated model that compacts curriculum in social studies.

In her heterogeneous class of 25 students, Mrs. Francis finds has identified four to seven students who could benefit from enrichment. She has profiled them as follows:

	Language	*Background Knowledge*	*Reasoning*	*Maturity (Sit-still-and-focus ability)*
Bradley	X	X	X	X
Kasey		X	X	X
Jonathan	X	X	X	X
Cynthia		X		X
Harmonie	X		X	
Emma	X	X		X
Darrow	X		X	

Map and Globe Skills

The third grade curriculum identifies the information, concepts, and skills for the map segment of the social studies curriculum as follows.

Students will demonstrate the ability to:

- ◆ Locate the following information on a map of a state:
  - ◆ Capital city
  - ◆ Home region
  - ◆ Major geographical features
- ◆ Identify the following on a globe:
  - ◆ Five continents
  - ◆ Four hemispheres
  - ◆ Four oceans
  - ◆ Major bodies of water in the United States
  - ◆ Islands

- Name and use the elements of a map:
  - Title
  - Legend (aka key)
  - Scale
  - Indication of compass direction
  - Symbols:
    - point
    - line
    - area
    - color
- Explain in their own words why maps must be specialized.
- Explain in their own words what kinds of information an atlas provides and how it is organized.
- Refold a road map.
- Identify various kinds of maps found in their homes, school, communities; in the newspaper; and on television.
- Translate information to express a base map as a thematic map.
- Use technology to find and use map information.
- Use local maps and road maps to plan basic routes.
- Draw a map of the schoolgrounds or neighborhood.

Initial Lesson: Whole Group Instruction

As Mrs. Francis conducts the following lesson, she pays particular attention to the seven students whom she is considering placing on an advanced level.

To generate interest about maps, Mrs. Francis has displayed numerous maps around the classroom. She orchestrates a class walk-around, noticing the level of interest that individual students express about the maps: *How closely are they looking? Where do they look first? What are they saying and asking? Are they making connections to background information?*

She then asks the children to tell what they've seen. She notices their level of interest and the accuracy of the language that they use to talk about maps. She asks them if they have any maps or globes of their own, if they ever helped their parents use a map, if they think they see maps every day, and, if so, what kind and what are they used for?

She then poses three questions and writes them on the board for think-pair-share:

1. How many different kinds of maps do you know?
2. How many maps have you seen in the last week?
3. What kinds of information can be given on a map?

After posting the information from the think-pair-share, Mrs. Francis solicits additional map vocabulary from the class: What other words do we use when we're talking about maps? She asks them to take all of the words now on the board and organize them into a tree-and-cluster diagram, reminding them that this kind of diagram is also a type of map.

The first abstract concept that Mrs. Francis wants to establish is the difference between two maps of the same place that give different information (types of maps) and two maps of two different areas that give the same kind of information (fields).

Mrs. Francis has gleaned a partial body of evidence about the candidates for the advanced grouping based upon her observations of them in this lesson and the level of thinking that they demonstrate on their concept maps. She will make her final decision after reviewing the following preassessment performance task:

> *"Now that we've looked at some maps and talked about maps, I'd like everybody to make a map of an imaginary place. The place could be a state or a country. It has to be big enough to have many cities, some bodies of water, and some of the other features that we talked about. Give your map as much information as you think it should have to make it useful, but don't give it too much information, or the readers will get confused. Make sure everything is labeled."*

Mrs. Francis evaluated the map-making performance task against the following criteria:

- Uses accurate terminology
- Shows an understanding of the kinds of information that maps can provide
- Has both details and generalities
- Has the elements of a map
- Shows a variety of features
- Shows understanding of the elements of social studies

She decided to compact the curriculum for four students, advancing them to more abstract levels of thinking about maps. She divided the class into five groups, four of which were heterogeneous, and one consisting of the advanced students. She gave each group a name:

The Trailblazers

The Pathfinders

The Explorers

The Third Rockers

The Navigators

She set up learning stations, as shown in Figure 5.1. At each station, the four heterogeneous groups did tasks that got the students used to working with maps and using map language. The advanced group worked on a more abstract level. Each group was given a small, color-coded adhesive marker to serve as their group's flag. Every child had a "traveler's journal" in which to write and/or draw what they learned at each station.

Figure 5.1

Activity 1

	Resources at the Learning Station:	*Heterogeneous Groups (Concrete to Abstract)*	*Advanced Group (Abstract)*
Station 1: Globes	Two globes and a wall map of the world	Locate the five continents and four oceans on both the globe and the wall map. (*Mark each with your group's flag.*)	What differences do you notice between the way landmasses appear on the wall map and on the globe? Why do you think these difference exist?
Station 2: State Maps	Four types of maps of the same state; atlas	What do all four maps have in common? How are they different?	Think of 4 other kinds of information that a map of a state could have, and draw rough sketches of two of them.
Station 3: Local Maps	Maps of the school district (one for each child)	Show where your house is located on the map.	Show the route that your school bus takes from your house.
Station 4: Language of Maps	Social studies textbooks	Look at the glossary of the social studies textbook. Find 20 terms that we use to talk about maps. Find examples of each term in the textbook maps, and record the term and the page in your travel journal.	Look at the glossary of the social studies textbook. Find 20 terms that we use to talk about maps. Find examples of each term in the textbook maps. Make a chart that shows the types of maps that each of these terms would be used for. Some terms will apply to all types of maps.
Station 5: Math of Maps	Social studies textbooks; math textbook; distance-measuring instruments	Mark the routes of two trips that you think would be approximately the same distance away from each other on the local map. Then, by referring to the scale and your measuring instrument, get an accurate measure of the distance of each trip. Compute the difference between the two distances. (*Remember, you need to travel on roads, not like a bird.*)	Suppose your mother has five errands to run on Saturday morning. Map out a route that will take her the shortest amount of time. Give her directions, including the distances between each point of her route.

Other Enrichment Activities

♦ *Maps and history:* Compare and contrast borders of European and African countries in the past 50 years.

♦ *Maps and stories:* Lots of stories involve maps. They may be hidden or discovered. They may reveal or conceal information. A character may have to read one map to get to another.

♦ *Maps and mysteries:* Research a real-life mystery involving a map. Think about underground maps, star maps, treasure maps, misleading maps, quests, and hunts for fugitives.

♦ *Maps and manipulatives:* Construct a three-dimensional map. Compete to assemble puzzles that represent maps.

♦ *Maps and metaphor:* Examine the symbols used on various kinds of maps.

♦ *Maps and movies:* Make a map that represents where your favorite movie takes place.

♦ *Maps and biography:* Use maps to tell the life story of an interesting person.

♦ *Maps and animals:* Show where various breeds of dogs or cats originate from.

♦ *Maps and work:* Think of all the different ways people have to use maps in various lines of work.

♦ *Maps and reading:* Read three storybooks that have pictures of maps in them. What do these stories have in common?

Remediation, Review, Reinforcement (RRR)

Mrs. Francis found that six to eight of her students had deficiencies in the skills necessary to proceed fruitfully through the learning stations. They were distracted, confused, disoriented, unproductive. She assembled a group of such students and had them do the following before moving back to the learning stations. But she also reassembled the other heterogeneous groups, to make the "RRR" group (named the Rangers) less conspicuous.

♦ *Too many maps.* The Rangers had to stay with one kind of map, the simplest one. She gave them a map of the United States, with just the outlines of the states printed. The Rangers began by identifying the states they knew. Using the wall map of the United States, they practiced visual transport by finding and marking major cities.

♦ *Not enough practice in using new concepts and terms.* Some of the map-learning language was foreign and intimidating to the children. They needed more practice in multi-syllable words such as *latitude, longitude, geographical, hemisphere, continent, peninsula.* Mrs. Francis helped them pronounce these words, using them in context and for a purpose. She created small tasks built around making visual associations, connecting the words to their corresponding images on the map. She reinforced their learning with mnemonics, but conceptual understanding was stressed over the mnemonic device.

♦ *Not enough background information.* Unlike some of the more culturally enriched children in the class, the Rangers stayed pretty close to their home ranges. They were not travelers, physically or intellectually. Lacking the schemata, the learning Velcro on which to stick new information about maps, the Rangers needed more time on the initial learning experience than Mrs. Francis had offered in her introduction to the whole class. These were children who hadn't contributed much to that lesson. As Mrs. Francis circulated around to the learning stations, she revisited those introductory words and images.

Maps and the Abstraction Ladder

♦ *For the RRR group.* Mrs. Francis wanted the Rangers to understand the difference between man-made borders and natural borders. From there, she had them differentiate between regions defined by geography (natural) and those defined by human decisions (man-made) of where a region begins and ends.

♦ *For the heterogeneous groups.* In transitioning from concrete to abstract thinking about maps, these students will discriminate between natural and man-made borders. From there, they will decide upon how they would divide a region not shown as divided on their map. From there, they will answer this question: *Aliens take over the state of Wisconsin. On their planet, all states are divided into 10 parts. How would the aliens divide Wisconsin into 10 parts? Why?*

♦ *For the advanced group:* Draw two maps having a similar design representing both abstraction ladders, as shown below.

1. Bessie	1. Main Street
2. Cow	2. Street
3. Livestock	3. Downtown
4. Farm Assets	4. Commerce
5. Assets	5. Business
6. Wealth	6. Civilization

Mrs. Francis's map lessons will be embedded into lessons throughout the year in all content areas.

- ◆ *Math:*
  Place value
  Carrying and borrowing
  Measuring time on clocks, calendars, timelines, schedules
  Measuring money: making change, different currency systems
  Estimating and rounding whole numbers
  Multiplication by single and double digits
  Division by single and double digits
- ◆ *Science:*
  Stages in the life cycle of animals and plants
  Relationships of Earth to moon and of Earth and moon to sun
  Expansion and contraction of water
  What energy is
  What molecules are
  The water cycle of Earth; water needs
  Basic functioning of Earth's ecosystem
  Adaptation of living things
  Nutrition and food groups; food hygiene
- ◆ *Social studies:*
  Social units
  Economics: production of goods and service; law of supply and demand; currency
- ◆ *Language arts:*
  Complete sentences
  Nouns
  Verbs
  Adjectives
  Common homonyms
  Capitalization
  Paragraph construction
- ◆ *Reading:*
  Main idea and details
  Conflict elements in a story
  Summary and retelling skills
  Visualizing descriptions

Math

Math Journals

In Mrs. Lee's fifth grade class, everyone keeps a math journal. There are three kinds of math journals:

The Writer's Math Journal

The Engineer's Math Journal

The Designer's Math Journal

When the class works cooperatively, sometimes the three groups work with each other. Other times, they count off by threes and mix themselves up, exchanging journals.

Mrs. Lee determines who does which kind of journal based on standardized test information, observation, in-class performance, and anecdotal information from parents and school personnel.

The Writer's Math Journal is for students whose verbal skills outweigh their math skills. The idea is to understand math one word at a time. The sections of their journals are as follows:

- *Vocabulary.* Keep a list of math terms learned in class. Use each term in a sentence about math. Your sentence must have an action verb (not *is* or *was*).

- *Sentence starters.* Write three to five sentences each day. Choose from this list:
  - I don't understand . . .
  - I still don't understand . . .
  - I'm finally beginning to understand . . .
  - I finally understand . . .
  - I know why . . .
  - I get confused when I get to the _____ part.
  - Another way I found to do this problem is . . .
  - Something new I learned today is . . .
  - I checked my answer by . . .
  - The clue to doing this problem is . . .
  - To do this problem, you have to know (how to) . . .

- *From numbers to words:* Write out the detailed process of doing a problem. Use "step language," which consists of words such as *then, after that, first, second, third.*

Mrs. Lee tells students who keep a Writer's Math Journal: "Sometimes, very good math students are good because they talk themselves through the math. You might notice your parents or other adults talking out loud to themselves as they work through a paperwork problem. You're good at words and sentences. Let your words help you."

- ◆ **The Engineer's Writing Journal** is for students who tend to be precise. Engineers are precise. They are comfortable with measurements. They concentrate well on lines, forms, things that fit together. The sections in their journal are as follows:
  - ◆ *Vocabulary.* For each term, make a labeled diagram that illustrates its meaning.
  - ◆ *Construction site.* Take several problems and show how they could be used to build something. Show a model of what you plan to build. Include measurements, and use proper measuring instruments.
  - ◆ *Encoding.* Pretend that a problem is the key to a secret hidden treasure. Express the problem using a code of symbols instead of numbers.

Mrs. Lee tells the group who keep Engineer's Writing Journals: "Think like an engineer. An engineer uses a kind of code in his drafts. You're good at numbers and measuring. Math problems area all about that."

- ◆ **The Designer's Writing Journal** is for students who have good art skills. Their door to math is their interest in shapes, symmetry, and relationships of things in space. The sections in their journal areas follows:
  - ◆ *Vocabulary.* Draw designs and figures that bring clusters of terms together.
  - ◆ *Three-dimensional designs.* Use your art skills to show how the math problems would look in three dimensions.
  - ◆ *Color.* Use color to show your understanding of the parts or steps of a math problem.

Mrs. Lee tells the group who keep a Designer's Writing Journal: "You can use your art skills to be better at math. Artistic people like you have a good eye for estimating the size of things, to picture things in different positions on the page, and to see how visual things would change if turned around."

Assessment

Mrs. Lee assesses by writing a limited and manageable number of questions and comments in the journals once a week, like this:

- ◆ What else?
- ◆ Can you think of other examples?
- ◆ Could you do this another way?
- ◆ You don't have enough written here. Why?
- ◆ You're on the wrong track here. Do you see where you went wrong?

- I can't read this. Can you help me?
- This is great. Can I show this to the class?
- You seem to get lost here. Can you see where?
- Do you need my help on this?
- What do you mean?
- Can you give more detail?
- Can you be more organized?

Students are expected to jot down brief (nonsentence) answers to the questions. They must use contrasting-color ink. When Mrs. Lee returns the journals, she spends time with pairs of students, helping them answer the questions that they can't answer for themselves. The next week, when she reviews the journals again, she'll look back at the answers from the previous week and put a pink sticky flag by the omitted answers, and a green sticky flag by the answers that show wrong thinking. "The journals get students to think of math as a form of communication. If they can communicate what they *do* understand, then it's easier for me to communicate to them what they *don't* understand."

The Dialectical Math Journal

An extension of the math journals described here is the dialectical, also known as the double-entry, journal. We see these most often as reader response. In math, it works like this: The student works through the problems on the left side of the page and concurrently writes commentary on the right. The commentary can consist of the following:

- Points of uncertainty
- Things that the student needs to keep in mind
- "This reminds me of . . ." statements
- Reminders of details
- Parallel problems
- Life applications
- Simplifications
- Rules
- Justifications
- Reasoning outline
- Anything the solver wants to do to think better on paper as she works through the problem

Linking the English Language Arts to Math

One way of strengthening both language skills and math skills is to show their common ground. This is differentiated instruction because some students will enter math through the door of language arts, while others will enter language arts through the door of math.

Entering Language Arts Through the Door of Math

Case 1: Lisa. Lisa has been classified has having language deficits. She struggles to put her thoughts into words. Though she's not a math whiz by any means, she does seem to have some strengths there that her learning specialist, Mr. Davis, thinks he can capitalize on. Lisa's immediate in-class needs in her mainstream fifth grade class are:

♦ Identifying nouns, verbs, adjectives
♦ Writing complete sentences
♦ Developing a paragraph from a topic sentence

It isn't hard to see that Lisa's sentence-fragment problem comes from thinking that a *which* clause should stand alone as a complete sentence. Many people think this, and you will even see it in print by respectable publishers. Nevertheless, Mr. Davis wants Lisa to understand that the *which* clause should be attached to the sentence that precedes it. Another type of clause that Lisa allows to stand alone is the *when* clause. *When* clauses usually need to be attached to the sentences that follow them.

Mr. Davis's strategy is to get Lisa to think about addition in writing: How are things added to sentences? He shows Lisa several examples from her writing folder of *which* and *when* clauses that need to be ADDED to the sentences before and after them, respectively. "Put a PLUS SIGN before *which*. Put a PLUS sign after *when*. Then, DO THE MATH and see if it makes sense."

To teach Lisa to identify nouns, verbs, and adjectives, Mr. Davis used math language that Lisa was comfortable with. He told her: "A noun is a word that you can ADD the word *the* to; a verb is a word that you can ADD the word *to* to; and an adjective is a word that you can ADD the word *truck* after."

Mr. Davis also taught her a substitution method: "If you can substitute the word *it* for a word (or words) in the sentence, then it is a noun (phrase). If you can substitute *do, does,* or *did,* then it's a verb (phrase). And if you can substitute *green,* then it's an adjective."

As for paragraph development, Mr. Davis worked with Lisa on the standard Harvard outline form, getting her to see that general ideas break down into smaller, subordinate ideas, the way numbers can be factored. He said, "What's inside the number? What's inside this big idea?"

Case 2: Justin. Justin is a star at math and science, and an above-average student in the verbal subjects. His teacher, Mrs. Cahr, wants Justin to be more challenged in math, to the advantage of his verbal skills. Mrs. Cahr devotes one instructional hour per week to in-class writing, assigning differentiated tasks. Over the years, she has built up a collection of dozens of topics that play into what she is teaching throughout the year.

Mrs. Cahr wants Justin to write a mystery story that is solved by mathematical sleuthing. His instructions are to use the skeleton of a mystery story that the class has read. He will replace the setting and characters with his own scenario, but the plot will be an adaptation of the original. The main clues leading to the solving of the mystery will require mathematical thinking.

Using Language Arts as a Doorway to Math

Case 1: Anya. Anya loves to read and learn new words, but numbers make her tremble. As a fourth grader, she's not fluent with her single-digit multiplication tables, so she's falling behind the class, which has started double-digit division. Her teacher has referred Anya to the math learning center in a pullout for two discretionary instructional hours per week.

Mrs. Sing works in the learning center with Anya and four other children. In teaching them the multiplication table for 6, she plays on their verbal skills: "Some of the "six times facts" rhyme," she says: "6×4 is 24. 6×6 is 36. 6×8 is 48." That may help, but it won't help for the entire table, so she shows them what she calls the "6 Secret." "The 6 Secret is that a lot of the multiples of 6 on the table make a "half" pattern. Look: 12, 24, 36, 42, 48, 63." This amount of knowledge will suffice for one session. Later sessions will fill in the 6 table: 6×5 will not be troublesome, because the 5's tables is automatic for these kids. The two remaining 6's from the single-digits, 6×3 and 6×8, can be learned through the 3 and the 8 tables.

To reinforce knowledge of the tables, Mrs. Sing does choral recitations, writing the numbers in both numerals and words, manipulatives, visualization, creative dramatics and role play, estimations, rhythmic speed drills, connect-the-dots, and number wheels.

Case 2: Katie. Katie needed to learn to talk to herself when doing math problems. She learned this, and it worked pretty well, but the trouble was she couldn't do this when taking tests. Katie's mom didn't want her to have a separate testing location, because Katie balked at the suggestion. So Katie had to learn to activate an internal monologue. She did this by using both her hands and her "head voice" to take math tests. Her teacher is working on getting her to feel more comfortable mouthing words while taking a math test. "Everybody else is busy doing their own tests anyway," she says.

Author's note: I'm like Katie. When I "do my taxes" or my insurance papers, I need lots of words. I need to talk, write, label, bundle, and color-code.

Other Language-Math Connection Strategies

- Kids make their own flash cards on colored index cards.
- Construct the Math Fact Zoo: Each species of animal has a diet of the multiples of a particular number. Give kids bags of number food (cardboard numbers) to feed to the animals.
- The more ownership kids can have in their learning of math facts, the more durable their learning is likely to be. Often, a student's own method will lead to more abstract math understanding, as it may be based on pattern making and logic, rather than rote memorization.
- Embedding math facts in a verbal context facilitates learning to do real-life math problems, which are always expressed with language.
- Always take advantage of Latin and Greek word roots to connect math language to conversational and literary vocabulary.
- "Read" a picture book for math: With each page, show what is happening mathematically in terms of shapes and sizes, proportions, and spatial relationships.

Summary

Abstract thinking is the big time. Difficult to teach as such and dependent upon readiness, abstract thinking is the line of demarcation between the primary grades and the mid-elementary grades. Some theorists posit that children aren't really able to think in abstractions until the age of 12. But our curricula demand some abstract thinking long before that. We differentiate instruction for abstract thinking by perceiving students' readiness, giving tiered assignments, using concept maps and graphic organizers to show abstraction levels, and moving toward abstractions gradually. As teachers, we need to understand when we transition from concrete to abstract, and we need to anchor abstractions with concrete examples.

6

Concept Mapping

Concept mapping is a way of showing connections, making associations, linking one idea to another. Concept maps can be used for all subject areas. In fact, concept maps are an excellent way to foster interdisciplinary thinking.

Research about how the brain learns, retains, and uses information shows us that learning is highly dependent upon associations; that is, the more integrated a given piece of information is into what is already known, the more likely it is for that new piece of information to make itself at home in the brain. That makes sense. If you go to a cocktail party and you don't know anyone, chances are you will linger around uncomfortably for a while and leave at your earliest opportunity. The event will be unmemorable. But if you know at least one person, that person may introduce you to others, and thus you become part of the scene. The same idea applies to acquiring new information. New information can be processed only if it can stick to old information. (If an "information bit" about chemistry were to wander into my brain, for example, it would die of loneliness. Nothing in my brain would recognize it or know how to use it. But when I learn a new fact about something that I love, like the history of the English language, my brain knows exactly where that piece of knowledge belongs in the context of the subject.). Thus, the more you know, the more you can learn. Knowledge builds capacity.

The strength of concept maps as a means of thinking and communicating lies in the fact that the mind jumps from one point to another more quickly than does the hand when writing sentences. With concept mapping, you have no superfluous words.

We may think some connections are obvious. We may make explicit connections to material already learned, thereby reinforcing prior learning. We may refer to cultural icons and familiar events in students' lives. However, we don't really know all that is in a student's experience. This is where differentiated instruction enters into concept mapping. We invite students to make their own explicit connections linking the new to the known. Because it shows understanding, concept mapping can also be used as alternative assessment.

You may hear concept mapping referred to as *mind-mapping, webbing, or radiant thinking.* Typically, a concept map is a representation consisting of circles and links, with the circles being nouns, and the links, verbs. The difference between a concept map and a flow chart or an organizational chart is that a concept map is freer, more flexible. A concept map may refine itself into a flow chart or an organizational chart, but the concept map is free and flexible, an *emergent* model of thinking. On the other hand, the flow chart or organizational chart is a finished product.

Thinking Through Concept Maps

Concept mapping involves nonlinear thinking akin to brainstorming. The difference is that with concept mapping, we are establishing relationships that is not established through brainstorming. Thus, concept mapping is a more structured activity.

Concept mapping allows us to view information all at once, from a viewpoint not available through a list. When we look at a concept map, we can see gaps, imbalances, contradictions, and overlaps.

Using the Concept Map as a Learning Device

1. *As a prewriting strategy.* There are two ways to use concept mapping as a prewriting strategy: brainstorming and organizational. A favored brainstorming map is the cluster map, consisting of burgeoning circles, each representing a possible idea and the subideas that it generates. Brainstorming requires lavish freedom of thought. For this, you need space. Colored markers on newspapers sheets and flip chart paper taped onto the wall work best.

The organizational plan prewriting strategy grows out of the cluster diagram. In the cluster diagram, the writer decides on main ideas, supportive details, transitional expressions, and keywords. The keywords unify the composition, appearing at least three times in three different spots.

To refine the organizational plan, writers can use stickers and stars to map out where certain strategic words are going to appear. For example, a social studies report is likely to have several proper nouns (names and places on the map), numbers (dates, ordinals, amounts), and visuals.

2. *To express hierarchy.* In learning about subordination and power structure, students construct hierarchy maps. Hierarchy maps show pyramidal organizations, such as those found in government. In a hierarchical map, you're looking for more than generalities and specifics, or classifications. You're looking for relationships in which upper-level units have dominion over lesser units. The military, corporations, schools, and the three branches of the federal government are good examples of hierarchical organizations.

3. *To show how a part-to-whole relationship works.* Maps representing part-to-whole relationships are used most commonly for math and science, but they are also useful for showing how words are built onto roots through prefixes and suffixes. We are accustomed to seeing part-to-whole relationships expressed in pie charts and bar graphs. We can also conceptualize part-to-whole by an "eyeball diagram." In this type of diagram, a smaller circle set within a larger circle indicates how a subgroup fits into a larger group. Another is the big-fish-eating-little-fish diagram.

4. *To facilitate memorizing.* We usually facilitate memorization with auditory modes and rhythm, but visual representation can also form associations. By making a concept map, students can establish pictures that can trigger memory. Memorized information will have more meaning and be more durable if the learner can find rhyme and reason. That's where concept maps come in. Real connections from one item to the next, rather than acronyms or mnemonics, will build learning capacity.

5. *To encourage class participation.* Everyone has taught classes in which a handful, if that, of students dominated while other students participated very little. Concept mapping gives students the think-time that they need, as well as some confidence when called upon. The Punctuation Map provides a structure for responding to information in four different modes: questions (?), surprises (!), statements of fact or opinion (.), and syllogisms (,), also called *if/then statements.*

6. *To develop an understanding of systems and sequence.* Students can draw concept maps to translate their verbal understanding of a system or sequence into a picture: a storyboard representing the process of long division, a diagram showing the relationship between velocity and acceleration, a framework illustrating how economic factors affect each other.

7. *To show rules and applications.* Rules of spelling and grammar are famous for their exceptions. Concept maps can reinforce which words are exceptions, with the added benefit that the exceptions themselves often form a pattern. In so doing, they become not exceptions to Rule A, but adherents of an emergent rule, Rule B. For example. the words *foreign, reign,* and *sovereign* are not just random exceptions to the *I*-before-*E* rule. They are a category in their own right.

8. *To make sense of readings.* After reading, we can use concept maps to recall, reinforce, and organize what we've read. It's best to do the map quickly at first, without consulting the material. Then the reader can go back to the text, filling in what was missed. To elaborate, the reader can use another color pen to add peripheral information and commentary. To strengthen the learning, ask questions about the map: Does everything fit together? Is anything missing? What are the repeated words? What are the opposites? How does this reading material fit into other knowledge? The same mapping procedure can follow a listening comprehension or class discussion experience.

Ways to Assess Concept Maps

We can think of concept mapping as a means for students to learn and a means for them to demonstrate what they know—an assessment. As an assessment, they can be judged based on the following:

- ◆ **Accuracy of relationships.** Are the relationships accurately named? Does the space interval between the items accurately represent the relationship?

- ◆ **Correct use of terminology.** It's a good idea to have terminology listed along the left side of the page. Advanced learners can compose their own list; emergent learners can complete a list that has been begun by the teacher; and beginners can have the list provided for them.

♦ **Detail and specificity.** Instruction in concept mapping is differentiated when students are expected to provide varying degrees of complexity. The degree of sophistication of the learning depends upon the refinement of detail in the map.

♦ **Overall organizational plan.** An exemplary organizational plan should be symmetrical, systematic, easy to follow, and simple in design. The design plan itself should not be so elaborate that it interferes with comprehension.

Teaching Students to Make Concept Maps

♦ To indicate relationships, use colors, clusters, arrows, shading, and branches. Think in terms of cloud diagrams (clusters of overlapping circles), tree diagrams, constellations (star patterns), and chains. Differentiated instruction moves toward having students find their own symbols and designs, ones that will be meaningful to them as individuals.

♦ Concept maps should be drawn quickly. The less self-editing, the better. To encourage nonlinear thinking, provide lots of space and freedom on the page. Leave white space to allow for ideas to develop later. Position the paper horizontally, and put the main idea in the center.

♦ Put the nouns in the circles, and the verbs in the connecting lines. If you want to include adjectives, cluster them around the nouns.

♦ Think in terms of Who? What? When? Where? Why?

♦ Think of the concept map as an emergent model, a work in progress. Revisit it often to add ideas and to make new spin-off maps out of secondary ideas.

♦ Print in capital letters to keep the points brief and readable.

♦ Use unlined paper. Lined paper inhibits nonlinear thinking.

♦ Generate lists from concept maps, and generate concept maps from lists.

As students learn and gain experience with concept mapping, and as their knowledge base grows, their maps will show more depth (greater detail) and complexity (more elements and relationships). Here is a guide for progressive teaching of concept mapping:

Beginners:

1. Begin by teaching that the most general concepts go in a deliberate place: on top, in the center, on the bottom.

2. Show completed models. Practice going from the written map to oral sentences, explaining their meaning.

3. Provide students with incomplete maps. For example, provide maps that present the verbs (links), and ask the student to supply the concepts (nouns). If students have difficulty, provide the list of concepts, and have them place them in the map.

4. Reinforce the vocabulary. Concept mapping assumes familiarity with the subject area vocabulary.

5. Practice going from general to specific. One way to do this with manipulatives in the primary grades is to sort picture cards into shoeboxes, where the shoeboxes are labeled with generalities, and the picture cards represent specifics.

Intermediate:

1. A more advanced approach is to present the list with no guidelines for the map. Students then have to determine what the hierarchical representation is going to look like and how they will express the connections.

Example: Make a map showing the connections between the following concepts:

> *city, country, town, village, state, province, county, parish, borough, township, subdivision, neighborhood*

2. You may want to include some peripheral concepts and tell the students that they can decide to leave some of the items out of their map.

Advanced:

1. The most sophisticated level of concept mapping is to give the students a general concept and have them construct their own map from scratch. This task requires thoughtful analysis.

2. Some children might be ready for this level but are intimidated by the blank page. You can bridge the intermediate and advanced levels by providing a modifiable tree diagram.

Increased Depth and Complexity:

1. Add examples.
2. Add synonyms and antonyms (in different colors).
3. Express the ideas on the map with oral and written language.
4. Make the map three-dimensional.
5. Work on symmetry, eye appeal, background/foreground, so that the map draws the viewer's attention first to the most important concepts and then leads attention to the subordinate ideas.
6. Develop maps progressively. Have the children keep their maps, refining them as they learn more concepts.

7. Refocus the map, showing a different angle or scope. Place a detail as the central concept and see what happens.

8. Include Venn diagrams in the concept map.

Modeling Concept Mapping in Whole Class Instruction:

1. Present a concept map at the beginning of the lesson to establish expectations.

2. Present an incomplete map at the beginning, and complete it as you go along.

3. Present the map at the end of the lesson as a visual and verbal reinforcer.

4. Distribute an incomplete map, and have students complete it as the lesson proceeds. This is a form of note-taking.

5. Construct the map along with the students as the lesson progresses. This is a way of checking for understanding and reinforcing concepts as the learning is taking place.

6. Call upon more capable students to construct maps as the lesson proceeds, and then have them explain their maps to the class. Students can use individual whiteboards, overhead transparencies, or a computer screen with projection capabilities to show their work.

Concept Mapping and Problem Solving:

In real-world situations, many workplace teams use concept maps to direct the problem-solving process. The keywords of the problem are centered on the page, with possible solutions and their ramifications radiating outward. Concept maps present possibilities, overview the problem, place the problem into a context, and invite involvement from the group members.

Once the problem-solving mind map is created, the group can form breakout teams to further explore the various quadrants of the map. The map can be color-coded in terms of the viability of the ideas generated. Connections may appear from one quadrant to another.

Concept Mapping and Cooperative Learning:

When children work together making concept maps, their conversations will be rich with content area language and words that signal higher-level thinking. You will hear them evaluating choices, justifying assertions, comparing, considering, defining, verbalizing abstractions. You will hear them asking interesting questions of one another. The social component of concept mapping promotes both reasoning and verbal ability.

Some teachers like to assign roles to students in cooperative learning groups. In a group of three children, one can be the Map Maker, one the List Maker, and one the Reporter. The Reporter explains the map to the teacher or the class. Additional roles can be the Wordsmith (spelling, definitions), Assistant Reporter, Keeper of the Facts, and various managerial roles (Timekeeper, Recording Secretary, Information Organizer).

To minimize frustration, the group will need an easily erasable medium on which to test ideas. Portable dry-erase boards work well. *Inspiration*® is a computer program that is specifically designed to construct all kinds of graphic organizers and outlines. It is very user-friendly and is also available as *Kidspiration*® for the lower grades. Concept maps can also be easily done through *PowerPoint*®.

Concept Mapping as Differentiated Instruction:

For concept mapping to work as differentiated instruction, not everyone's map should be expected to look the same. Children should have the freedom to do more than just fill in circles with a given list. Even when a list is provided, students should be encouraged to augment the list with their own ideas.

As a bridge between verbal and nonverbal forms of intelligence, concept mapping plays into learning styles.

Concept Maps and Reasoning

Inductive Reasoning

Inductive reasoning is the process of making generalizations based on particulars. By looking at commonalities among examples, we infer that these examples will apply to other cases, and we draw a conclusion. That conclusion may be known as a *hypothesis*, a *rule*, a *maxim*, or a *generalization*, depending upon the language used in the subject area. (In science, we refer to *hypotheses;* in English grammar, we refer to *rules*.) Inductive reasoning speaks of classes, saying: "If this property applies to part of this class, then I induce that it will apply to the whole class, until proven otherwise."

We engage in inductive reasoning all the time. As thinkers, we need to act upon our reasoned generalizations, while simultaneously maintaining an open mind: Our generalizations must remain subject to revision.

When students are given the chance to reason inductively, they are doing field research. They *discover* truths for themselves, rather than being told what is true. Inductive reasoning works particularly well in matters of English usage and spelling. You can lead students to understand the rules of capitalization and punctuation by having them first gather evidence in real text and then draw conclusions as to the rules. This is differentiated instruction because you can assign varying levels of reading sophistication to students. Figure 6.1 shows an inductive reasoning map.

Deductive Reasoning

Deductive reasoning is the reverse process of inductive reasoning: Beginning with the generalization, we generate specifics. We say: "This is true of most cases. Therefore, it probably applies to this specific case." Whereas the

Figure 6.1

Inductive Reasoning

Observation:
Observation: Hypothesis:
Observation:
Observation:

Figure 6.2

Deductive Reasoning

Example:
Principle: Example:
Example

inductive reasoner goes from minor to major, the deductive reasoner goes from major to minor.

The famous *if/then* syllogism is deductive reasoning: *"If* all American citizens are entitled to due process, *then* Americans abroad are entitled to due process." To teach from deductive reasoning, we would ask student to find examples, given the template of the rule or generalization. For example, students would look for examples of the "*I*-before-*E*" rule. Figure 6.2 shows a map of deductive reasoning.

Matrices

Matrices, usually applied to math, can also generate differentiated instruction in social studies, language arts, and science. We place the generalities on one axis and the specific on the other. Matrices can be used to differentiate instruction because they offer choices, as follows:

- ♦ Students can complete the entire matrix or parts of it. The matrix can be presented with some of the squares filled in.
- ♦ Students can supply the specifics on the vertical axis.
- ♦ Students can get to point where they create their own matrices for a subject area.
- ♦ Because they are rich in information, matrices can form the basis for written work.

Four examples of how matrices can be used to differentiate instruction are described below.

For Example 1, an animal matrix, students select the animals that they wish to describe. You can give the task more depth by requiring students to provide more specific, detailed information in each square. You can give it more complexity by having students choose animals that share an ecosystem.

Example 1

Animal Matrix

	Habitat	*Diet (and how it gets its food)*	*Means of Protection*	*Locomotion*
1.				
2.				
3.				
4.				

Example 2, a grammar matrix, has students examining authentic language in search of specified grammatical classifications, in this case, kinds of nouns. This task differs from the exercises in traditional grammar books because, in those books, the language is controlled so as to display certain characteristics. The task may be differentiated if the teacher distributes texts in varying levels of sophistication.

Example 2

Grammar Matrix

	Concrete Nouns	Abstract Nouns	Collective Nouns	Proper Nouns
Page _____				
Page _____				
Page _____				
Page _____				

For the vocabulary matrix of Example 3 to be differentiated, the students would choose words from their text (or some other language source) that they would like to know more about.

Example 3

Vocabulary Matrix

Word	Meaning	Used in a Phrase	Has a prefix	Has a suffix

The geographical features matrix of Example 4 shows how geographical features affect key life-style features of their regions. To differentiate this activity, students can choose particular regions of the world, or they can elaborate on the information in the squares.

Example 4

Geographical Features Matrix

	Deserts	Mountains	Islands	Plains
Economics				
Food Supply				
Climate				
Transportation				

Other Concept Maps

Here is a list of relationships that concept maps can show:
- consistency
- connectedness
- continuity
- sequence
- orderliness
- lineage and order of succession
- gradation
- rank
- series
- transformation
- progression
- rotation
- priorities
- alternatives
- cycles
- stages and transition
- procedures
- design plan
- perspective
- attributes and qualities
- proportions
- chronology
- possibilities
- issue/problem/suggestions/solution

Summary

Concept mapping (also called by many other terms) is a means for encouraging nonlinear thinking in all subject areas. Because it allows for free thought and a variety of responses, it is one of the tools of differentiated instruction. In the primary grades, concept mapping works well because it can be done with pictures and with single words, rather than full sentences. Concept mapping can be done individually, with pairs or teams, or as a whole class activity. It permits children to use large areas of space, such as newsprint, chalkboards, and dry-erase boards. Excellent software (*Inspiration*®, *Kidspiration*®, and *PowerPoint*®) is also available for concept mapping.

7

Teaching Question-Making

Not all differentiated instruction models divide kids into groups. When we teach students how to ask all kinds of questions, that is another form of DI. It is a powerful study and review strategy that has many applications for critical thinking, reading comprehension, and cooperative learning. We will consider four kinds of short-answer questions:

◆ Multiple-Choice
◆ True/False
◆ Matching Columns
◆ Sentence Completions

Teaching Students to Write Objective-Type Questions

Mr. Quinones teaches fourth grade. Because of state-wide high-stakes tests given in the fourth grade, he needs to be very conscious of test-taking skills. He has found that teaching students to compose test questions satisfies the need for differentiated instruction and constructivist, active learning, while at the same time preparing students for traditional tests.

Multiple-Choice Questions Based on Reading Comprehension of Fiction

Let's begin with the much-maligned yet perennial multiple-choice question format. Typically, each question has four choices, with one correct answer and three distracters. One of the distracters should be immediately rejected by the student who is fairly well-oriented in the subject. We need this choice to appear, to signal to us that a student is seriously far from the mark.

The Question Templates in the following discussions provide a base upon which to create multiple-choice questions.

Meaning of a Word in Context

- **Learning theory.** Mr. Quinones teaches students to be aware that a word means only what it means in context, that a word may be used metaphorically, that its meaning may be narrowed or extended. Recognizing that a word may be used differently from subject to subject is an extremely important critical thinking skill, the skill of mental flexibility. When Mr. Quinones' students are making these kinds of questions, they are looking for two kinds of words: those whose meaning they wouldn't know in isolation, and those whose meaning they know, but the context is using the word in a divergent way.

- **Directions to the students.** *A word can have different meanings, depending on how you use it. Find a word that is used in a way that is different from what you are used to. Ask the reader what this word means in the way that it is used.*

  Or:

  When we read, we meet new words. Often, we can figure out what new words mean because of clues in the sentence and paragraph. Find a word that you think your classmates might not already know, but that they can figure out by reading carefully.

  - Question Template:

    In paragraph 4, the word _____ means:

Main Idea

- **Learning theory.** The ability to discern the main idea from supportive detail is one of the most important reading skills a reader can have. This type of question is favored by reading comprehension tests from elementary school to the SATs. Consciousness of main idea is an essential habit of mind for readers. This applies to the piece as a whole, as well as to paragraphs.

- **Directions to the students.** *Whenever we read, we always have to keep an eye on the main idea. The whole piece has a main idea, and each paragraph has its own main idea. The main idea of a paragraph is usually stated in one sentence, called the* topic sentence. *The topic sentence usually appears as either the first or the last sentence of the paragraph. Ask a question that wants to know if the reader understands the main idea of the whole piece or one paragraph.*

  - Question Templates:

    The best title for this piece would be:

    The author's main idea is about:

All of the sentences in paragraph 2 tell about:
The topic sentence of paragraph 3 is found:

Sequence

- ♦ **Learning theory.** A nonchronological narrative requires the reader to pay attention to sequence words: *before, after, then, later.* More sophisticated stories have more exposition (events that occur before the curtain of the story goes up). On the sentence level as well, complex sentences tend to cover more than one time zone. The developing reader reaches the next level as she learns to handle nonsequential text by mentally reordering events.

- ♦ **Directions to the students.** *As you read, pay attention to what is happening when. Not everything happens in the order that you read about it. Make questions that help the reader understand what is happening first, second, third . . .*

  - ♦ Question Templates:
    The event that happens before the story begins is:
    Which of the following events occurs first:
    The story takes place over _____ days (weeks, months, years).

Prominence

- ♦ **Learning theory.** The careful reader understands the difference between major characters and events and minor ones. She has a sense of background and foreground as she reads. Although some details may be more interesting to the reader than the main ideas are, skillful readers know how to subordinate details to the main ideas.

- ♦ **Directions to the students.** *Some things are more important than others in what we read. Write a question that helps the reader put some characters and events in the background. To find background features, ask yourself what could be left out of the story for it to still make sense.*

  - ♦ Question Templates:
    Which of the following does the author want you to pay the most attention to:
    If you had to take one of the following out of the story, it would be:

Orientation

- ♦ **Learning theory.** The reader has to know where she is relative to the story: Where is the story taking place at given times?

- ♦ **Directions to the students.** *When you read, you should place yourself inside the story. Look around and see what's there. Travel with the story. Write a question that helps readers think about where the story takes them.*

◆ Question Templates:

The weather in the story is:

The story takes place in the season of:

The story begins (where?):

The middle of the story takes place (where?):

The story ends (where?):

Inference

- **Learning theory.** The ability to read between the lines, interpreting what is *not* said as well as what *is* said, is abstract thinking, and thus a sophisticated skill for an elementary student.

- **Directions to the students.** *When we read, we need to pay attention to what the author is hinting at. The author may not tell us that a character misses her mother when she's away at summer camp, but the author shows us a scene where she's looking at her mother's picture and taking it with her wherever she goes; she may be talking to her mother in her mind, or rushing to collect the mail every day. From this information, we can figure out without being told that the character is sad without her mother. Write a question that helps the reader understand something that the author does not come right out and say, but that you can figure out by the clues.*

    ◆ Question Templates:

    We think:

    We think this person wants:

    We think this person feels:

Fact and Opinion

- **Learning theory.** Discerning fact from opinion is a critical thinking skill necessary for making judgments. In the elementary grades, students should be introduced to rhetorical signals that indicate opinion, such as first-person point of view, strong emotional language, and language indicating preference.

- **Directions to the students.** *Sometimes, what you read is totally factual. Facts are information that you can look up somewhere else and they would be the same. And sometimes, authors are writing to give their opinion, to tell you what they think about the facts, or whether they think the facts are even really true. Write a question that helps people understand the difference between facts and opinions.*

    ◆ Question Templates

    The passage consists of:

    a) all facts.

    b) all opinion.

c) some facts and some opinion.

Tone (Author's Attitude)

♦ **Learning theory.** Discerning tone is a mature and subtle reading skill. But if kids can tell when you are angry, when you are trying to be funny, when you are serious, and when you are frivolous, they can begin to understand what tone is in what they read. Faltering readers are too busy decoding and putting meaning together to perceive tone. Rather than using the term *tone*, which is quite abstract, you can refer to the author's feelings in the elementary grades.

♦ **Directions to the students.** *Let's think about how the author feels about _____. What words and sentences tell us how the author probably feels about this subject? How do you think the author wants you to feel about it? How do you know?*

  ♦ Question Templates:
  When the author wrote this, you think he(she) felt:
  The words that show that the author is (angry, sad, smiling) are:

Relationships

♦ **Learning theory.** Understanding relationships brings in the skill of inference-making. Concept maps assist the reader in seeing relationships among characters. To get kids to think about relationships, make a list of all the interpersonal relationships they can think of. Organize the list in terms of those in which people are equal and those where one person has authority over the other. Role-play dialogues that indicate the type of language used with various relationships.

♦ **Directions to the students.** *Think about the characters and how they know each other. Which characters are the bosses? Do the characters live together? Are they meeting each other for the first time in the story, or have they already known each other before the story began? Are they polite to each other? How do you know?*

  ♦ Question Templates:
  The characters _____ and _____ are (name of relationship):
  Two characters who dislike each other are:
  Two characters who trust each other are:

Cause/Effect

♦ **Learning theory.** In helping students understand cause/effect, we need to be careful not to ascribe a causal relationship to a merely sequential one. (We think of the anecdote of the farmer who thought that the rooster brought the dawn in.) Graphic organizers are often used in teaching cause and effect. In reading, the signal words are *because*, *therefore*, and *this is why*.

- ◆ **Directions to the students.** *In books, just like in life, things happen for a reason. Think of the most important things that happen in this story. Why do they happen? What causes them? Make a question that helps readers understand how something happened.*
  - ◆ Question Templates:
    _____ *happened because . . .*
    _____ *caused . . .*

Author's Purpose

- ◆ **Learning theory.** Like tone, perceiving the author's purpose is a sophisticated skill. It involves a rudimentary understanding of the different rhetorical modes in terms of what language can do: *persuade, describe, entertain, evoke emotion, explain, narrate*. To teach these modes, the reader must have a sense for the intended audience.
- ◆ **Directions to the students.** *What do you think the author wants you to think or feel after reading this piece? Do you think the author is expecting someone your age to read it? Do you think the author expects you to learn something? What? Do you think the author expects you to enjoy this? Laugh at it? Feel some emotion because of it?*
  - ◆ Question Templates:
    Most of the people who would read this are probably:
    The author wants you to read this because:

Author's Assumptions about the Reader

- ◆ **Learning theory.** Similar to knowing the author's purpose is psyching out what the author thinks about the readers: How educated are they about the subject? What knowledge are they assumed to possess? Are they likely to be reading this on their own, in pursuit of their own interests, or are they probably reading this because a teacher assigned it?
- ◆ **Directions to the students.** *What do you think this author knows about you? Does she know how old you are? That you are reading this in school? What does she think you already know? How can you tell?*
  - ◆ Question Templates:
    The author probably thinks you are:
    The author thinks you already know about:
    The author thinks you don't know about:

Multiple-Choice Questions Based on Experience and Observation

For the discussion in this section, refer to Figure 7.1, which lists the steps in constructing a battery.

Figure 7.1
Procedure for Constructing a Battery

Step 1: Fill a container with vinegar.

Step 2: Place strips of cloth into the vinegar. Swish them around. Remove them and wring them out to remove the moisture. Lay them out flat on a work surface.

Step 3: Take a piece of copper and a piece of zinc, and put the cloth strip between them.

Step 4: Repeat the above so that you have four units.

Step 5: Make a stack of the four units. Wrap the stack with aluminum foil.

Step 6: Connect the battery to the light. The light should go on.

Sequence of Steps in a Procedure

♦ **Learning theory.** In this active-learning science lesson, students need to follow an orderly set of directions. They watch a demonstration and then replicate it. The task involves visual, kinesthetic, and reasoning ability.

♦ **Directions to the students.** *Now that you've seen and done the procedure, how much of it do you remember?*

   ♦ Question Templates:
   Which of these steps is out of order?
   Which ingredient is used first in the following pairs?

Words in Context

♦ **Learning theory.** One way of being science-smart is to understand how technical language differs from the vernacular, even though the sounds and spellings of many words may be the same. This requires mental flexibility—the ability to suspend one's notion of what a word means in one context and apply the same word to another context. Usually, the words do not bear their meanings randomly. Often, the scientific application of the word bears a metaphorical connection to the vernacular.

- ♦ **Directions to the students.** *We said that we needed to dip the cloth in the vinegar because the vinegar makes the cloth a conductor and an insulator. But where else have we used the word* conductor? *Does it mean the same whenever it is used? How do we figure out what a word means if it means something else in a different sentence? Make a question that helps people understand that words can mean different things in different subjects, depending on the words around them.*
  - ♦ Question Templates:
    When we talk about _____, the word _____ probably means:
    A word that we've used in this lesson that can have another meaning is:

Assumptions and Inferences

- ♦ **Learning theory.** Science is dependent upon assumptions and inferences and, at the same time, is skeptical about them—hence the constant need to prove things for oneself, to replicate conditions and procedures to see if the same result is obtained.
- ♦ **Directions to the students.** *In science, things happen that we can't see. We can't see the molecules reacting to each other to make a current. We can see only the result of the closed current: the light going on. Make a question that shows people what they are assuming about things that are going on that they can't see.*
  - ♦ Question Templates:
    How does the vinegar bath change the cloth?
    At what point is the circuit closed?
    What would happen if the circuit was not closed?

Materials Present

- ♦ **Learning theory.** Observing materials and calling them by their proper names are essential science skills. These words may be unfamiliar to children, so you may have to exaggerate and emphasize the words for the tools and materials of science.
- ♦ **Directions to the students.** *We've used some materials here that you may not have seen before. Write a question that helps people remember what these materials are called and how they are used to make the battery.*
  - ♦ Question Templates:
    The metals used to make the battery are called:
    The type of liquid used as a conductor and insulator is called:

Multiple-Choice Questions Based on Reasoning

For the discussion in this section, refer to Figure 7.2.

Figure 7.2

Number Table

16	32	28	16
24	24	28	28
16	32	32	24

Sequence (What Would Come Next)

- **Learning theory.** Predicting the next item of a series or filling-in a missing item in a series is an essential reasoning skill because it involves comprehension of how a pattern is put together. Often, we lead up to this skill by showing visual patterns, such as wallpaper and wrapping paper.

- **Directions to the students.** *Look at the number table. If the number table were to be extended in a "going down" direction, what numbers would come next in each column? Make a question that helps people find out what numbers would come next.*

  - Question Templates:

    What do the numbers on the vertical axis have in common?

    What do the numbers on the horizontal axis have in common?

    Which of the following numbers is most likely to appear on this number cube?

    Which of the following numbers is least likely to appear on this number cube?

Compare/Contrast

- **Learning theory.** An essential part of pattern-finding is recognizing similarities and differences. To compare and contrast the numbers on the table, students have to consider multiple ways of categorizing and ordering numbers.

- **Directions to the students.** *Look at the numbers on the number table. What do all of the numbers have in common? Think of as many ways as you can to show similarities in these numbers. For every way that they are alike, though, they must be different in some way. Write a question that gets people to find ways in which the numbers on the horizontal and vertical axes are alike and different.*

♦ Question Templates:

What number would have to pair up with 24 for it to have the same relationship as 16 and 32?

Which columns should be paired together because they have the most in common?

Process and Procedures

- ♦ **Learning theory.** Processes and procedures refer to the verbs of number manipulation: *add, subtract, multiply, divide, reduce, factor, equalize, estimate, round.* Given a number table students can perform various operations.

- ♦ **Directions to the students.** *Write the number 4 in the center of your paper. Think of all the operations you could perform (all the things you could do) to the numbers on the number table to get 4. Write a question that gets your classmates to do the procedures necessary to get 4.*

  - ♦ Question Templates:

  What would you do with _____ and _____ to get a sum of _____ ?

Estimations and Expectations

- ♦ **Learning theory.** Estimating is an important habit of mind in tackling number problems. When we have an estimate in mind before doing a calculation, we have our wits about us and are less likely to commit a gross error.

- ♦ **Directions to the students.** *You get into the car with your family. Where are you going? You probably picture your destination in your mind. The same is true for a math problem. You have some idea of what the answer is going to look like. We call that an* estimation. *Some people call an estimation a* ballpark figure. *Write a question that helps people get a ballpark figure of their answer before they start.*

  - ♦ Question Templates:

  The sum of _____ and _____ is probably not more than:

  The sum of _____ and _____ is probably not less than:

If/Then

- ♦ **Learning theory.** The "if/then" syllogism is a staple of logic, involving the mental manipulation of variables and understanding of consequences. We can establish a syllogism and then abstract it into a mathematical statement. This can be translated to mathematical language: *If P, then Q. It is P. Then it is Q.*

- **Directions to the students.** *In understanding how the world works, we need to understand that things will happen if certain conditions exist. One way of expressing this is with the "if/then" statement: If it rains on Tuesday, then we will postpone our field trip. It is raining on Tuesday. We will postpone our field trip. That may seem easy to you, but let's change it a little What if I say: "If it rains on Tuesday, then our field trip will be postponed. It is not raining on Tuesday. Our field trip is not postponed." What's the problem here? Well, maybe it's snowing on Tuesday. Maybe our field trip is postponed for some other reason. Write a question that helps your classmates understand an "if/then" statement.*
- Question Templates:
  Which of the following "if/then" statements are true?

Terminology

- **Learning theory.** Math has its own language. In fact, there are those who say that math *is* a language. Math terminology offers the perfect opportunity to teach that words change depending upon the context. Math terms are often a mouthful and have Latin or Greek roots. This means they have lots of relatives in their word families, lots of teaching opportunities by association.
- **Directions to the students.** *Let's help each other speak math. Lots of math words mean something else when we use them in another subject. And lots of math words are a mouthful to say and tricky to spell. Write a question that helps your classmates speak math like a native.*
- Question Templates:
  The _____ in a math problem means:
  The word _____ is related to:

Writing True/False Test Items

You can differentiate instruction by having students compose true/false statements, because they will compose statements at varying levels of complexity. The true/false test, still a staple of short-answer tests, is not as easy as it seems because it requires a "mental flipping" of information processing. Also, the reader must consider both the main clause and the subordinate clause, or other tacked-on grammatical structures, to determine the truth or falseness of the statement. As the reader's/listener's attention is drawn to the main clause, there could be another "falsifier" in the sentence that goes unnoticed by the not-so-careful reader/listener.

Many true/false statements contain negations (*not*) in them. It takes the brain longer to process a sentence presented in the negative than in the affirmative form. In the true/false statement that contains a negation, the student has to process the negative *and* determine its truth: a double process.

General advice: True/false test-takers are generally advised that polarizing words, such as *all, none, always,* and *never,* usually signal a false statement, while qualifying words, such as *probably, usually, sometimes,* and *often,* usually signal true statements. Teach students to approach T/F items with the mindset that the statement is true unless proven otherwise. They should section off the statement to determine that each part is true. It's a good strategy to circle the part of the statement that makes it false.

Writing Matching Columns Tests

Matching columns are a kind of game. They are good for testing knowledge of simple identifications, definitions, key features, famous people matched with their achievements. To have children make their own matching tests for each other, provide the template, as well as a word bank from which to choose test items.

To differentiate the matching column task, advanced students can do the following:

- Compose sentences out of the matched pairs.
- Take the matched pair, put it together, and compose another matching column to link the newly made matched pair.
- Decide upon an organizational plan for the matched pairs, and put them in some kind of order.

Struggling students can be helped in the matching task if you do the following:

- Give them not more than five items at a time to match.
- Supply verbs to connect the nouns in the matching column.
- Provide a wider range of difference between the items.
- Match nouns to nouns.

Writing Sentence Completion Tests

When students make their own sentence-completion questions, they need to determine the keyword in the sentence to be replaced. The sentence-completion item can be a fill-in (constructed response, where the student pulls the words out of her own mind), or a multiple-choice answer, or an answer taken from a word bank.

For more able students:

- Have them write their own sentences.
- Have them omit more than one word in different parts of the sentence.
- Use the constructed response method.

  For struggling students:

- Provide the sentence and have them decide which word to omit.
- Combine a form of multiple choice by offering two possible words to complete the sentence.

Summary

Having students make up their own questions is an effective means of differentiating instruction, especially for teachers who are uneasy with group-work or who think their particular classes will not function well without heavy structure and individual accountability. Although constructivist learning theory usually eschews traditional tests in favor of performance tasks, having the students themselves compose questions indeed requires a higher-level thinking skill that has the advantage of making students better test-takers in the process. Question-making is a focused, purposeful way for learners to apply information and understand what how tests tick.

8
Differentiating Instruction for English Language Learners

I am the best of them that speaks this speech/Were I but where 'tis spoken.
William Shakespeare—The Tempest, Act 1, Scene 2

One of our biggest challenges in differentiating instruction is teaching students whose native language is not English. These students range from those who enter our schools knowing no English at all, to those whose speech is proficient but whose writing lacks the fluency of a native speaker. Unless you have been trained in TESOL, you probably don't know much about how to address the needs of these students. This chapter will consider four questions:

1. What do you need to know about your ESL students?
2. How are other languages different from English?
3. How do differences in dialect affect learning?
4. How can you help?

What Do You Need to Know about Your ESL Students?

To work with students who are learning the English language, we first need to understand some rudiments of second language learning. Then we need to consider some basic facts in comparative linguistics. The purpose of this chapter is to help you make your English language learners more at ease and better able to communicate with you. Here are some questions about individual students:

♦ **How closely is her native language related to English?** English is a Germanic language with Latinate and Greek influences. It is cousin to the Romance languages: Spanish, Portuguese, French, Italian, and Romanian. The ESL student whose native tongue is a Romance language will find many cognates that open doors to English words. On the other hand, Asian languages have much less common ground in terms of sentence structure, word order, formation of plurals, and the sounds themselves. Asian languages have very few cognates for the student to hang her hat on.

- **What is her functional level as a speaker of English?** In the best of circumstances, your school will have an ESL specialist who will evaluate the English proficiency of your students and give you an accurate report.

- **How old is she?** Before puberty, language is learned intuitively, in the left hemisphere of the brain. After puberty, we lose the ability to learn language intuitively, and language learning becomes a right hemisphere function, more difficult to keep in long-term memory.

- **Is she socializing with English speakers? What is the language of her socialization?** Anything you can do to encourage socialization in English would be helpful. If you've ever been in a country where you don't speak the language, you know how lonely and frustrating it can feel. Schools that care about their ESL students arrange for social opportunities such as clubs, buddy systems, breakfasts, and invitations to events. They see to it that their community welcomes newcomers and makes a place for them. Teachers who care about their ESL students express an active interest in their culture and language, offering opportunities for them to communicate and make friends, making sure everyone in the class knows how to pronounce their names, presiding over an atmosphere of invitation and inclusion.

- **Is she happy to be here?** Affective factors play an important role in second language learning. Aversion to a culture, not wanting to be here, longing for home and family, all can impede learning English. These students need adults in the school to look after them. Sad to say, sometimes our ESL students are exploited as laborers and are not given time and opportunity to study.

The first and best way to differentiate instruction for your ESL students is to be a gracious host or hostess to them in your classroom. The other students will follow your example. Learn all you can about their interests, their level of proficiency, their family situation, their culture, and their language. Doing so will make the situation less frustrating and more rewarding for everyone involved.

Finally, a remark about the word *foreign*. If you lived in a place and went to school there, would you want to be considered a "foreigner"? *Foreign* and *foreigner* are words that should be consigned to the list of archaic and misguided epithets that we don't use anymore in polite society. Spanish, for example, is hardly "foreign" in the United States. It is one of many languages spoken in a society where English is the predominant language.

How Are Other Languages Different from English?

Some of the following information may be too specific and grammatical for your needs. The purpose of this section is to show you some basic differences in structure between English and several other languages: Spanish, Hmong, Vietnamese, Cantonese, and just a dash of Japanese and Korean. This information is not meant as a crash course in six languages. It is hoped that by knowing some of the ways in which your ESL student is struggling to make sense of English, you can better support her.

Spanish

Perhaps the most glaring difference between Spanish and the other Romance languages and English is that the Romance languages genderize their nouns. A Spanish-speaking student may take a while to get the hang of using the neutral pronoun for inanimate objects. Additionally, English nouns don't necessarily take an article (*a, an, the*), whereas Spanish nouns usually do. Spanish speakers may want to insert an article before nouns that don't take articles in English, and this may sound very odd to us.

In Spanish, as in many other languages, the adjective usually comes after the noun. In English, the adjective is usually in the pre-noun position, but it can also be a predicate nominative, that is, a word that follows *to be*: *Martha is silly.* In English, the adjective means the same thing whether it is in the pre-noun position or the predicate nominative position. However, in Spanish, the adjective changes meaning when it appears in the pre-noun position (which is seldom). In English, we don't pluralize our adjectives; in Spanish, we do pluralize adjectives.

Don't be surprised if your Spanish speakers conflate the prepositions *in, on, at.* They are accustomed to using one preposition (*a*) for all of these meanings. You'll hear your Spanish speakers use *that* when you expect *who* or *which.* The reason is that Spanish uses the word *que* to refer to *that, who,* and *which.*

Spanish speakers don't like to end a sentence with a verb. You might hear them switch the subject and verb in a sentence that comes out sounding awkward in English. Instead of *I know what she is thinking*, you may hear or read *What she is thinking I know,* or *She is thinking I know what.*

English has only one verb for the *to be* concept, but Spanish has two be verbs: *ser,* for permanent circumstances, and *estar,* for temporary ones. In English, the direct object comes after the verb, but in Spanish, the direct object comes before the verb. English places the indirect object between the verb and the direct object. *Jack sent Jill a pail of water.* Spanish places the indirect object between the subject and the verb: *Jack Jill sent a pail of water.*

In English, when we refer to a person, we use the same language whether that person is present or absent. But Spanish speakers use the article to refer to an absent person. In English, that would sound like this: *I saw the Mrs. Benjamin in the grocery store.*

You may hear Spanish speakers refer to the word *people* in the singular rather than the plural. The reason is that *la gente* is singular in Spanish.

Spanish expresses the person that the verb refers to by manipulating the ends of the verb. This is called *inflection,* and it is a hallmark of the Romance languages. Because the person (first person, second person, or third person) is implied by the verb inflection, Spanish speakers are free to omit the pronoun altogether. We never do this in English. Your Spanish-speaking ESL student may think that it is acceptable to omit the pronoun in English.

In English, we express possession in one of two ways: We use the possessive apostrophe or the *of* phrase. The Romance languages use only the *of* phrase. Considering how much trouble native speakers have with the possessive apostrophe, you can imagine how much trouble a Spanish or French speaker would have with it.

Hmong

Hmong, a language spoken in Southeast Asia, has a complicated system of noun classifiers to introduce nouns. In English, we use very few noun classifiers: *a, an, the,* and some possessive pronouns. In Hmong, there are hundreds of classifiers, and each has to match a particular classification of noun. Hmong speakers may insert superfluous noun classifiers in English.

Because Hmong speakers form the possessive by using a noun classifier that is not available in English, they may be confused by the possessive apostrophes. They may also be confused by the apostrophe in English contractions.

The passive voice of the verb is not available in the Hmong language. Verbs are always expressed in the active voice. This may present problems in reading and listening comprehension because the student may wrongly interpret an English verb in the passive voice, thinking that whoever is meant to receive the action is actually performing the action of the sentence.

Hmong speakers are used to keeping the form of the pronoun the same, whether it is in the subjective or the objective position. In English, the pronoun changes from subjective case (*she*) to objective case (*her*) depending on its relationship to the verb.

Another area of confusion for Hmong speakers may be the use of *what* in question formation. Hmong speakers employ the word *puas* to form a question; they do not use end punctuation to mark a question.

Hmong speakers don't use the verb *to be* when using a predicate adjective in a sentence such as *He is cute.* They would say: *He cute.*

Finally, the Hmong language pluralizes by inserting *cov* before the noun. The practice of pluralizing by adding *s* to the end of the noun will be unfamiliar.

Vietnamese

As in Spanish, the Vietnamese adjective is placed after the noun. Vietnamese does not have the *to be* verb. You can expect your Vietnamese students to need help inserting the correct form of *to be* in statements and questions.

A writer of a sentence in Vietnamese will usually place a transitional word between the introductory clause and the main clause. In English, this sounds awkward: *Because she likes to sing, therefore she joined the choir.*

Vietnamese, like English, uses the subject/verb/object order. However, Vietnamese omits *it* when referring to weather, distance, and time. There are no neuter pronouns in Vietnamese.

In English, we express comparison by adding *er* to the adjective (*bigger*). In Vietnamese, the concept of *more* is expressed by adding the word for *more* after the adjective: *The truck big more than the bus.*

The vowel sounds in the words *hit, bad, shower,* and *hire* are not heard in the Vietnamese language. This accounts for why the Vietnamese speaker may confuse words that sound like words that have these vowels.

Expect your Vietnamese students to have some trouble with tense. Vietnamese does not use the same system of expressing events in time. You might hear and read: *We take a trip to Sacramento last summer.* This speaker is using context clues in the sentence to convey the tense, rather than transforming the verb, which is what we do in English, but not in Vietnamese.

Cantonese

Cantonese speakers are not accustomed to using helping verbs for questions or negatives. They may be particularly baffled by the English use of *do* in questions and negatives. You may hear this: *How much money this cost?* When we speak English using a helping verb, we usually don't stress that helping verb, so it would be hard for a native Cantonese speaker to hear it. You may want to stress the use of the helping verb *do* in questions and negatives.

Cantonese speakers are likely to be confused by the use of prepositions in English because Cantonese does not use many prepositions. Prepositional use in English is so idiomatic that it may even seem to be random. For example, why do we ride *in* a car but *on* a train? Why do we park *in* the parking lot? Why do we hang a picture *on* a wall, rather than *against* a wall? Your Cantonese speakers may need you to emphasize prepositions in your speech, to help them hear the conventions.

You'll hear your Cantonese speakers placing all of their modifiers up-front in the sentence, before the verb: *For her mother on her birthday on Saturday, we gave her a surprise party.*

Cantonese speakers tend to leave off plurals in English because of the nature of the Cantonese grammar and also because of their difficulty in pronouncing the final *s*.

Cantonese speakers may have trouble with pronouns. They are used to a language with fewer pronouns, many of which are dropped.

A, an, and *the* are not used in Cantonese. That is why Cantonese students may erroneously omit the article, as in: *I have dog.* They may also insert the article erroneously, as in: *I have the pets.*

Korean

In Korean, pronouns don't have gender, so you might hear Korean-speaking students referring to males and females using the gender-neutral pronoun *it.*

Japanese

In Japanese, pronouns don't have to match their nouns in terms of singular or plural, so you might have to show them how to use *we, us, they,* and *them.*

General Strategies for ESL Students

Students whose native language is not English don't automatically know how much English depends on word order for meaning. Although you take for granted that *The dog bit the man* conveys a different meaning from *The man bit the dog,* an English language learner might not think that the difference is so obvious. English is a subject/verb/object language. Japanese and Korean are subject/object/verb languages. Arabic is a verb/subject/object language. Knowing this difference may help you decipher your students' intended meanings as they learn English.

Because English is a word order language, it's important to understand what a direct object does. A direct object receives the action of the action verb. In the English sentence *Claudia loves Ramon,* Claudia, the subject, is giving the love; Ramon, the object, is receiving it. This is what we mean by the SVO (subject/verb/object) pattern.

In English, we expect the subject to be stated (except in the case of commands, where the subject is "you (understood)." Many other languages do not require that the subject be stated outright but expressed through the verb ending. You may have to remind students that in English, the subject must be stated first. English language learners need to stick to simple SVO sentences.

One more fact about verbs: The most common verbs in English are the irregulars, a fact that is not convenient for fledgling speakers.

In English, we place the preposition before its object. That's why it's called a *pre*position. Other languages don't necessarily have this placement. Sometimes, the object comes before the preposition.

Talking about transportation is often a puzzlement for English language learners because of the prepositions *in* and *on.* When the vehicle carries only one person, or when it carries more than a handful of people, we use *on: on* a bicycle, *on* an ocean liner, *on* a train. When a small number of people ride in a conveyance, we use *in: in* a rowboat, *in* a car.

English language learners may need some help understanding the meanings of conjunctions, so you might have to explain the difference between *and* and *but.*

In English, it's easy to form the past tense and past participle, because both forms are the same for regular verbs. All we do is add *have* or *has* to the past tense to form the past participle. Not all languages work this way.

English is rich in metaphors, idioms, and figurative language. You can imagine how these nonliteral expressions would bewilder the novice. An idiom such as *used to* is famous for mystifying newcomers to English.

Remember that conventions for capitalization differ from language to language. Nationalities are not capitalized in Spanish, Romanian, Russian, or Portuguese. The second word of a geographical place name (*Hudson River*) is not capitalized in Serbo-Croatian and Vietnamese. Not all languages capitalize days of the week or months of the year. Cantonese does not use any capital letters to indicate a proper noun.

Not all punctuation looks like English punctuation. Some languages use inverted questions marks, circles, vertical lines, series of dots, and other markings Commas don't always appear the way they do in English. In some languages, the comma is inverted, raised, or reversed.

Not all languages have the same rules as English does regarding the joining of independent clauses. Whereas English does not permit two independent clauses to be joined by a comma, such joinings are permissible in Persian, Arabic, Russian, and Turkish.

English spelling drives native speakers crazy. Imagine what it must be like for speakers of languages such as Spanish and Vietnamese, which have much more consistency. Your ESL students will run into difficulties that you don't expect, because their pronunciation conventions may differ from those of English speakers. For example, in some languages, the final consonant is not pronounced. If a speaker of such a language carries that practice into English, she will be likely to drop the final consonant in spelling as well as in speech in English words.

In English, we have lots of affixes. Other languages, such as many Asian languages, do not add affixes to words very often. The notion of a word root, which has meaning although it does not function as a complete word, is unfamiliar.

Your non-native speakers will have enough problems with the irregularities of English spelling. You can help them learn spelling by working with them on their pronunciation. Doing this doesn't always require correcting them. Simply exaggerating your own pronunciation of tricky words will be helpful.

Chinese and Vietnamese do not pluralize words. These languages convey the plural in the context of the sentence. Romance language do have plurals, but the plurals are formed according to rules that are much more consistent than the rules in English. Be aware that ESL students may find English plurals difficult.

Homonyms, words that sound alike but have different, often unrelated, meanings, don't exist in all languages.

Finally, we need to keep in mind that the nonverbal cues of communication differ from culture to culture. Most Americans expect the person to whom they are speaking to make eye contact. Not to do so is considered a sign of disrespect. In some cultures, making eye contact is a sign of confrontation; downcasting one's eyes when an authority is speaking signifies proper deference.

How Do Differences in Dialect Affect Learning?

One of the goals of education should be to make every high school graduate bidialectical. Everyone has a dialect. By *dialect*, we mean speech patterns that are at variance with the homogenized style of public discourse. We can think of this as "private speech" and "public speech." Some linguists refer to "private speech" as "the language of the family." You may also think of bidialecticalism as "informal" and "formal" language.

Enlightened educators appreciate and value all of the many forms of spoken English, and they recognize the various voices of informal written English. At the same time, it is incumbent upon us as educators to help our students communicate in a way that will not put them at risk of being thought unsophisticated when they travel from place to place or from level to level in the business world.

This is a sensitive area. Nothing is more personal to us than our language and the language of our family, loved ones, ethnic group, and community. It is imperative that we show and feel a genuine respect for dialect. It also behooves us to know something about the grammatical structures of the dialects that we hear in the communities in which we teach.

One of the most controversial English language variants is AAVE (African American Vernacular English). In *Understanding English Grammar*, Martha Kolln and Robert Funk explain the use of the *to be* verb in AAVE. The way the *to be* verb functions in AAVE is actually more refined than in so-called Standard English, because AAVE distinguishes between present action which is going on now (*He eat*) and habitual action (*He be eating*). Before we judge a dialectical variant as "substandard," we need to know more about its grammatical structure.

We suppress dialect at our peril, as our suppression feeds a sense of alienation from education and public discourse, the last thing any educator wants. The classroom task is to establish the relationship between voice and audience.

In English, social studies, and language classes, we can differentiate instruction by acknowledging dialect in authentic literature and documents. We can show changes in the language over regions and time.

How Can You Help?

- To help ESL students learn how to use nouns and adjectives, have them write descriptions.
- To help ESL students learn how to use pronouns, have them write narratives about themselves and their friends.
- To help all students become more sophisticated about dialect, avoid using terms such as *substandard, wrong, broken English, illiterate,* and other pejorative terms that discount the value of linguistic variation.

Instead, use terms such as *colloquial, informal, regional, dialectical,* and *inappropriate for this context.* Stress the importance of using the language tone geared for a particular audience and situation.

♦ To help all students learn more about languages, point out cognates and Latin roots. This will also help native English speakers learn and remember new words.

♦ Find as many ways as possible to reword complex statements.

♦ Use visuals, but explain them verbally.

♦ Be responsive to the affective needs of new students.

♦ Be aware of the effects of your speech. Speak more slowly than you ordinarily would. Gesture and use facial expressions to exaggerate your meaning. Use the active voice and positive statements. Speak in short sentences.

♦ Be aware of context, and include definitions of unfamiliar terms within your sentences.

♦ Be aware that the English language is full of idioms which baffle the novice.

♦ Organize your message around keywords, and use them frequently.

♦ Model a positive, open-minded attitude about language variations. Doing so is one of the most powerful ways that you can teach for social justice.

How We Learn Another Language (Including English as a Non-Native Language)

The language learner must become an observer and an imitator:

♦ By imitating what she hears: emphasis placed on spoken, rather than written, speech.

♦ By following auditory observation with imitative oral speech: This would include the social circumstances under which certain ritualistic words are said.

♦ By hearing and practicing ritualized language: poetry, songs, proverbs, sayings, slogans, stories.

♦ By fusing word to meaning: linking sound to its concrete or abstract referent.

♦ By engaging in conversations in which the verbs are manipulated; by using correction through modeling.

♦ By using lots of pictures, especially pictures that show social interaction.

♦ By hearing and saying grammatical patterns and sentence templates.

Summary

Here are some of the ways that languages can differ from English:

♦ The nouns can be genderized.

♦ Plurals may be formed by adding words or syllables to the sentence, or by giving context clues in the sentence to indicate that there is more than one.

♦ The word order may not follow the familiar subject/verb/object pattern.

♦ The pronoun may not have to agree in gender or number with its antecedent.

♦ Other languages may have fewer prepositions, making it confusing for the novice to know which preposition to use in English. Also, the preposition may not precede its object.

♦ There are differences in inflection and pacing.

♦ There are differences in written conventions, such as punctuation and capitalization.

♦ Nonverbal communications, such as gesture, eye contact, silences, and what people do to indicate that they understand, differ from culture to culture.

9

Differentiating Instruction Through the Arts

Any discussion of differentiated instruction, learning styles, brain-based learning, multicultural education, educating for social justice, and multiple forms of intelligence must include the arts. In her article entitled "Gaining the Arts Literacy Advantage, Laura Longley (1999) reminds us that the world we live in and are creating for the future is

> . . . beyond global. More complex. Faster. Ambiguous. Visual. Virtual . . . Tomorrow's world will demand a quick mind. Focus. Discipline. Imagination. Grasp of the big picture. Attention to detail. Teamwork. Knowing good work from bad . . . How will we educate our students to thrive in such a world? Through the arts.

Technical proficiency does not suffice to build leaders and people adaptable to change. The young people whom we send out into the world need divergent and convergent thinking. When they learn the arts, they think verbally and nonverbally, symbolically and literally.

Integrated arts education has brain-based learning research behind it. It is through multisensory experience that we remember things, make them real. Through the arts, we can assess students in multiple ways, accommodating diverse learning needs. Through the arts, we make connections, remember what we've learned, extend our thinking. The arts teach us not only how to communicate complex ideas, but also how to formulate them.

Here are descriptions of what various districts are doing to integrate the arts to differentiate instruction (Longley, 1999):

- ◆ Las Cruces, New Mexico: Bonnie Hosie is an elementary visual arts teacher. When she wanted to teach kindergarten children about the color wheel, she had them mix colors in finger paint. She tells of one child's revelation when, looking at his orange hands, he "got it!": Red and yellow actually and literally and miraculously MAKE ORANGE! She would see this little five-year-old look at his hands weeks later, remembering the color wheel. What a wondrous example this is of literally having learning in your own hands.

- ◆ Miami-Dade County, Florida: In a school district that integrates the arts into reading, writing, and mathematics learning strategies, fifth graders use a sketchbook/journal to work out their ideas. For example, the children went on a field trip to an art museum, where they viewed works related to the First and Second World Wars. This was in the context of a unit on conflict and resolution. The children then learned about conflict and resolution through interviews with adults, stories, and historical events. All the while, they used their sketchbook/journals to express what they thought about and what they knew. These sketchbooks were such a powerful artifact attesting to what children think about human relations that the Wolfsonian Museum actually purchased them and put them on display in its permanent collection!

- ◆ Milwaukee, Wisconsin: Twenty-five private and parochial schools and the Milwaukee Symphony Orchestra have an education partnership called *Arts in Community Education* (ACE). The partnership seeks to advance every student's learning through a series of culturally diverse arts presentations and experiences. These presentations and experiences center on a theme at each grade level, K-12. The program includes problem solving, science and the arts, the blending of cultural influences as seen in the arts, and local and global community formation through the arts.

- ◆ Maine Township, Illinois: Park Ridge High School believes in the performing arts and creative writing. They offer a wide array of courses in speech, drama, broadcasting, creative writing, art, photography, and music. Here is what their curriculum guide says:

  [The arts] teach students where to look and what to look for in gathering support for an idea. They also help students learn to give, to accept, and to follow constructive criticism; listen courteously and critically as others speak; become more logical, more direct, and more creative in organizing thoughts for presentation; learn to control the fear of speaking or performing before an audience, and, as a result, become a more confident person. (President's Committee on the Arts, 1999, p. 61)

At Park Ridge, they include the arts in their assessments of all seniors, requiring exit tests in one field.

Art is about big projects with a lot of moving parts: producing a play, presenting a concert or dance recital, constructing a visual arts portfolio, writing a book. Such projects encompass emotional and intuitive as well as academic intelligence. Students involved in the arts learn about coherence, cause and effect, critical thinking, decision making, self-understanding, and communicating with others.

Here are the comments of Hewlett-Packard's Doug Sessions after his visit to the new School for Arts and Academics in Vancouver, Washington:

> [T]he interdisciplinary approach to instruction, the project-oriented focus, the sense that students are working in teams, collaborating, and, too, the high expectations in terms of the core subject areas, that's something that comes through. You know, you don't have to be here very long to see that there's an ethic of high performance. It's kind of an unusual place for Hewlett-Packard to look for math and science achievement, but the whole package is here. That's what we want. That's the way our employees work. (President's Committee on the Arts, 1999, p. 33)

The term *whole package* is the key to realizing the importance of integrating the arts into the school day. The arts bring in communication, culture, cognition, and creativity. This chapter suggests integration of the arts, not merely add-on after-school programs or "enrichment" time in the arts. The arts have tremendous potential for maximizing learning in a differentiated classroom. The proven benefits of arts integration far outweigh budgetary objections. We need to prioritize what works.

Eleven Ways to Facilitate Community Supports for Arts Integration

1. Do research that shows the importance of the arts.
2. Garner community support.
3. Use that community support to educate the BOE and the administration.
4. Institute block scheduling.
5. Write grants.
6. Be prepared to show proven results.
7. Connect the arts to social justice and violence prevention.
8. Enlighten your school community about multiple intelligence theory.
9. Showcase the arts.
10. Hire teachers who have a background in the arts.
11. Encourage, fund, and facilitate field trips to museums and concerts.

It is through the arts that we make the emotional connections so important to learning. The arts offer opportunities for interdisciplinary problem solving, verbal and nonverbal communication, and socialization.

We know that healthy brains flourish in an environment rich with sensory input, beauty, and rhythm. The arts strengthen memory, critical thinking, and neurological synapses. The arts are manipulative, cognitive, emotional, and social. Creating a work of art requires decision making, revision, reflection, patience, and knowledge of traditions and technique. The artist needs to know physics, mathematics, engineering. Through the arts, we travel, know other cultures, understand the past and how it prologues the present. That which can't be expressed in words can be expressed through the arts.

Humor and the Arts

There's a reason why the words *humor* and *human* sound alike. To the Greeks, "humors" of the body referred to various internal fluids. We don't have to go into detail here about these fluids and what each was associated with. We just have to think about how human it is to have humor, how essential humor is to being human.

The arts offer lavish opportunities to bring humor into the classroom. And the reason we should want to do so is simply this: Levity enhances learning. Laughter promotes fellowship, reduces stress, induces trust. It may even increase the body's production of neurotransmitters that sharpen alertness and memory. The following are some media or activities that integrate the arts with humor:

- Videos
- Role-playing
- Cartoons
- Satire
- Music
- Games

The ability to make people laugh is an intuitive blessing. People who are funny can't help being that way. It's their worldview that others find surprising, outrageous, ironic, incongruous.

You can't order or assign students to be funny, but you can allow them to have fun and to learn through humor. Gary Larsson was a biology teacher. One way that he had of teaching biology was to make zany cartoons, which developed into *The Far Side*. All those amoebas and protozoans, those guys in lab coats bending over specimens, those multi-tentacled sea creatures, struck Larsson as absurdly funny, given the right context.

Six Reasons to Bring the Arts to Your Classroom

1. The arts help students understand, remember, and construct information.
2. The arts are about science; science is about the arts.
3. The arts can be used to make academic information real for students.
4. The more interdisciplinary connections students can make, the better they will retain and value their learning.
5. The arts allow for multisensory learning.
6. The arts bring multicultural education to academics.

Advertising, Arts, and Academics

We should not overlook advertising as a hub for various art forms: poetry, music, visual arts, and drama. Advertising is accessible to students. It's their common cultural touchstone, and we can exploit that common knowledge.

For example, consider slogans. Everyone knows that slogans are memorable and durable. When we learn history, we learn lots of slogans and metaphors that have poetic qualities: *Operation Desert Storm, Operation Infinite Justice, the Dust Bowl, the Cold War, the Red Scare.* What about slogans in science? *An object in motion tends to stay in motion. For every action, there is an equal and opposite reaction.* We think of these as principles, and they are, but they are also slogans. We remember them because of their poetic qualities. Suppose students were to dramatize a science commercial ending with an overvoice of one of their slogans. Using props, dialogue that uses the language of science, and demonstrating a principle, they would not only be learning themselves, but they would also be instilling a memorable visual and auditory image in others.

How is using slogans to learn science or history a way of differentiating instruction? Use of slogans allows students to connect new knowledge to prior knowledge, making sense of the unfamiliar by means of the familiar. It validates the cultural capital that they bring to the classroom. Not everyone will do the same thing with the same information in the same way. That's differentiated instruction.

Sometimes we scoff at the demands that we "make learning fun." We get frustrated with this idea because we know that learning a complex body of information can't always be fun. We are teachers, not recreational directors. Besides, "fun" gets old fast, and then it's up to us to come up with more "fun." Meanwhile, there's a Big Test out there, and it isn't going to be any fun to take it. True enough. But that doesn't mean that we should trivialize the importance-the *educational* importance-of enlisting pop culture on the side of conveying information.

Advertising involves music. Music is memorable. We often remark that students who can't remember multiplication tables or presidents have no trouble with song lyrics. Maybe they could remember information if they set it to the tune of a familiar song.

Reflection

1.   Your students bring to your class a great deal of information based on advertising. How can you use this information to strengthen learning in your classroom?

2.   How do slogans play a part in learning in your classroom? How can you make more use of slogans?

3.   How do you already integrate the arts?

4.   What are some ways in which you can strengthen learning in your classroom by integrating arts education?

Arts and Critical Thinking

♦ The word *artist* is used generically to refer to various people who create things of beauty and power. Make a concept map to show the various kinds of "artists" and their relationship to each other.

- Make a concept map that shows as many categories of the arts as you can think of, including the relationships among them.
- The official language of ballet is French; the official language of music is Italian. Make a poster that illustrates some commonly used terms.
- Try to express in words why you don't like your parents' music and why they don't like yours.
- Compare movies to plays.
- Compare watching a movie at a movie theatre to watching a movie at home.
- Suggest a tale as a Disney movie.
- What does an artist have to know about science? What kinds of artists have to know the most about science?
- Think of five movies. Do the characters in these movies speak English in a different way than you do? How is their way different? Why is it different?
- Make a scrapbook of photographs that represent the past year in America.
- What does a photographer need to know about math?
- How many different kinds of music can you think of? When you make a list with other people, there may be some kinds of music that you have never heard of. Ask your teacher to help you find that kind of music to listen to.
- Interview someone who was born in another country. Ask her what she misses most about that culture. Ask her if/how she experiences her home culture in America.
- Find reproductions of several paintings of urban (city) scenes and several paintings of rural (country) scenes.
- What are the most famous museums and concert halls in the world?
- Finally, how has the September 11 disaster affected the arts in New York and in the world?

Feng Shui and Differentiated Instruction

What Is Feng Shui?

Feng shui is the Chinese way of thinking about how objects are arranged in an environment so that you feel most energized and peaceful in that environment. Feng shui enthusiasts believe that gaining control of their homespace and workspace will give them a sense of orderliness, energy, and peace. They believe in the psychological power of possessions, not necessarily for their material value, but for the emotional solace that certain treasures can bring: the memories, the beauty, the associations.

I discovered the feng shui philosophy recently, and I believe it to have some interesting potential for differentiated instruction because it is about self-understanding, personal decisions, organization, forming criteria against which to evaluate things, and caring for one's belongings. It develops the aesthetic sense of finding beauty in ordinary things and finding beauty in the perfection of order and organization. Feng shui is anti-clutter and anti-carelessness. It encourages a civilized, thoughtful relationship between people and their stuff.

One more reason to teach American children about feng shui is to bring in Eastern thought. Showing how other cultures view the home is a living lesson in social studies. As with all fields, feng shui comes with its own vocabulary, its own maxims, its own new ways of looking at the world, which is what the social studies are all about.

How Can You Learn More about Feng Shui?

Do a little browsing on the Internet, but don't be put off by the New Age and religious language you may run into. I recommend the *Personal Paradise Cards* by Terah Kathryn Collins. Her approach to feng shui is based on home organization and arrangement. If you're the type who loves home decorating, you may really enjoy this in your classroom and at home.

How Can Feng Shui Be Used for Differentiated Instruction?

1. Reorganization of the classroom. I'll give you a Chinese saying: *If you want a change in your life, move 27 things in your house.* Positive material changes just make you feel better in your home, and the same is true of your *other* home, your classroom. First, simplify. Throw things out with abandon. Victoria Moran advises us in her book *Shelter for the Spirit* that you can't organize excess! Things that you keep should be the things that love and serve you. After you've chosen the things that love and serve you, make them accessible to be loved and used. Clean them and the drawers and shelves that house them. (Now, aren't you feeling better just thinking about this?)

2. What you need for a peaceful and productive environment. Here are Terah Kathryn Collins' suggestions:

   ♦ For a sense of health and life, have plenty of healthy plants displayed. Teach the children to care for them and love them.

   ♦ For beauty and color, have some pots of dried or silk flowers displayed on bookshelves and on your desk. Have the children take care of them by dusting them.

   ♦ To show the beauty of work and what humans can accomplish, have lots of beautiful (but inexpensive and nonfragile) art to look at: pictures, ceramics, sculptures, basketry, textiles.

♦ To show love of the people in our lives, have lots of photographs of the loved ones of the children and yourself. Display these with the caring they deserve.

Remember that the purpose of the feng shui efforts are to make your classroom *more inviting* to the people for whom it exists: children. But I'm betting that the time and care you take to arrange a beautiful and orderly environment will pay off in uplifted morale for you and your students.

3. Encourage thoughtful "space care" habits. Make it a deliberate part of daily routines to care for the classroom environment. Make time to put things away, to clean things that look musty, to organize the personal learning space, to sharpen up the school supplies, replace shabby book covers. Mind follows body: The more we care for the things of learning, the more we come to value learning itself, and the more we consider the classroom a treasured space.

When you differentiate instruction, you start to build learning centers. Make sure they are visually conducive to the kinds of activity you want in the centers. In a reading center, you may want pictures of quiet, natural scenes, books having inspirational quotations, photographs of people to be admired. In a center where action, such as creative dramatics, is to take place, you may want white and primary colors, lots of natural light, whimsical and colorful things, lots of boxes with props.

4. Differentiated instruction applications. Students can try these:
   ♦ Go home and organize your room. Then describe in writing, or through diagrams or photographs, how you did it.
   ♦ Interview an organized person. Ask her how she stays organized.
   ♦ Write 10 reasons to stay organized.
   ♦ Organize your backpack. Make a written plan to have it stay organized.
   ♦ Move 27 things in your house (with your parents' permission). Write a report about what you did and why. (Moving parents, grandparents, or siblings is not permitted.)
   ♦ Find a friend in the class whose room you can go into. Make a partnership oral report comparing the two rooms.
   ♦ If you have home decorating magazines handy, describe how some of the rooms are arranged to make them beautiful.
   ♦ Take a field trip to a store that specializes in home and office organization. There's a whole world of vocabulary in these stores and a lot to be learned about classification. Encourage divergent thinking about how some of the containers and organizational systems can be used. Ask them where certain items should be placed.

Author's Note: Although the ability to create an organized and beautiful environment is an admirable quality, remember that this skill comes with great difficulty to some children and adults. Avoid using words (even in referring to yourself) like *slob, pigsty, a mess.* For some people, orderly placement of things in the environment takes practice and modeling. It's a mistake to assume that someone can organize by just by having the will to do so.

10
Paradigms for Differentiated Instruction

This chapter is about how various contemporary paradigms work. A *paradigm* is a complex model that holds a set of beliefs, in this case, about education. The one-room country schoolhouse was a paradigm, as are the finishing school for young ladies, the military academy, the "reform school," and the boys' prep school where boys wear navy blazers and the principal is called the *headmaster.* The Catholic school of my youth, with habit-garbed, ruler-wielding nuns, is a paradigm, as is the high-ceilinged urban classroom of the first half of the twentieth century, with its forty-odd desks bolted into rows. In the 1960s, suburban towns boasted low-swung centralized high schools servicing thousands of students with courses like home economics (then called *homemaking,* for girls only) and industrial arts (then called *shop,* for boys only). Home schooling, with its reliance on the Internet or its fundamentalist Christian ideology and skepticism about "government intervention" in public schools, is another paradigm, not so new but fervent and gaining ground.

We read books like this to transition into new paradigms. The ones described here, not surprisingly, are informed by research in how children learn and relate to each other in humane ways. The paradigms are the following:

- ◆ Brain-based (aka "brain-compatible") learning
- ◆ Multiple intelligence
- ◆ Sensory learning styles
- ◆ Brain laterality
- ◆ Thinking styles
- ◆ Metaphors
- ◆ Puppets, Masques, and Make-up

Guiding Principles in the Brain-Based Learning Paradigm

To illustrate the DI applications of the brain-based learning paradigm, we will use the field of spelling instruction. This discussion is based on the work of Caine and Caine (1997).

Simultaneity

The brain is a parallel processor. Think of how the camera's eye sees the entire picture within the frame. The brain takes in ambient sensory input. This is why memories flood in when you hear a particular song, eat a particular food, or smell a particular odor. Just as a sensory input brings back memories of the context in which that sensory experience was lived, we learn "everything at once" in our environment. That is why a child who takes a test in the same classroom in which she learned the material can read all kinds of invisible cues from the environment in which the material was learned.

Spelling applications:

- Couple spelling instruction with other sensory input, so that children make the immediate association between, for example, the taste of licorice and the suffix rules.
- Teach children to "read invisible letters." Have them recall words that were posted in some way but are no longer visible: What color was the word? Where was it? What was around it? What was going on when that word was posted?

The Everything Effect

Relatedly, everything that the body, mind, and heart experience affects learning: physical comfort or discomfort, stress, nutrition, lighting, all kinds of sensory stimuli, exercise, cultural background, fear, gratification, sense of safety, relationship to others. The instructional implication of The Everything Effect is that we need to understand that there are factors affecting learning that are out of our control as teachers. Nevertheless, we can consider teaching as an act of *hospitality*. We do well to make the sensory environment as conducive to learning as possible. Sensory input in the classroom is not a frill: It enhances or impedes learning and retention.

Spelling applications:

- Give students some choice and control over their spelling list and how they learn it.
- Encourage awareness of how success in spelling was achieved. Teach students how to replicate conditions of success: *What happened that worked for me? How can I make that happen again?*

Meaning-Seeking

The human brain seeks to make sense, to create order out of chaos. To make sense of things, we categorize, name, connect. To do these things, we practice the Sesame Street® game of "One of These Things Is Not Like the Other." We find sameness and differences. Think about how important this is. It is through discerning similarities and differences that we make meaning out of almost everything we know. We generalize from one case to another, find exceptions, figure out where new things belong, define concepts, apply rules, all based on how we figure that "this" is the same as or different from "that." Think about what Supreme Court Justices do: Aren't they matching cases to the Constitution, sorting out what's the same and what's different?

Spelling applications:

♦ English spelling is not chaotic, as is sometimes thought. Words, by and large, are spelled in accordance with how they *used to be pronounced* in England. Knowing this makes spelling seem more like the organized system that it is than an unfathomable jumble of arbitrary rules.

♦ Why teach spelling words one at a time? All words are related to other words. Always teach spelling in word clusters. Give every word "friends" and "relatives."

Pattern-Finding

An extension of the "same and different" search for meaning is that the brain makes meaning by finding patterns. A pattern is a repeating and predictable cluster.

Spelling applications:

♦ Use colors, shapes, wheels, folded paper, columns, bunches, bundles, and other patterns to show word clusters.

♦ Use wallpaper books, quilts, and fabric to show patterns. Design letters that like to go together into decorative patterns. Make a "spelling quilt" out of letter and word clusters.

Emotions and Patterns

Our own attitudes and experiences determine the patterns that we discover. To differentiate instruction, we need to show students how to use their emotions to find patterns and make connections.

Spelling applications:

♦ Find spelling patterns and word clusters in the routines of daily life, in the weather, in calendar lessons.

♦ Notice phases of the moon and patterns in the night sky. Instill a sense of order, restoration, renewal, and redemption in the patterns of life and the universe. Make a letter sky, forming constellations out of letters that like to go together.

Simultaneous Processing of Parts and Wholes

One of the fiercest controversies of the past two decades in education is between phonics and whole language instruction. A related controversy involves "writing process" versus "explicit grammar instruction." Both sides are about the relationship between the parts and the whole. But when we encamp ourselves too firmly on one side or the other, we fail to understand that the brain processes part and whole simultaneously. The best research on reading and writing instruction favors an integrated, differentiated approach, wherein the student learns both the parts (phonics) and the whole (text) simultaneously. This is how musicians and athletes have always learned their crafts.

Spelling applications:

- ◆ After learning a phonics rule and doing patterned practice, go on a spelling safari in real language, scouting out examples of the words that follow the rule just learned.
- ◆ Make semantic collections of words that like to go together to talk about certain subjects. Then find phonic partners for these words.

Concentration and Peripherals

While students are learning the main event, they are also learning from the stimuli around the room, such as the side conversations and peripheral images zipping about. Picture yourself walking down a busy city street. All that peripheral information registers in your consciousness. That is why you can be thinking of a certain word and then see that very word right in front of you in a store window. Without realizing it, your mind picked up that word and brought it to the foreground of your thoughts.

Spelling applications:

- ◆ In filling the room with words to read, include past, present, and future: words we've seen before, words we're seeing these days, words we will see in the future.
- ◆ Never deliberately present the incorrect model. Tests in which the students are asked to select the correctly spelled word among misspellings inadvertently convey erroneous information, especially if the misspelled words are typed. The brain automatically imprints a typed word as "correct."

Conscious and Subconscious Learning

Because we process peripheral information, we learn much more than we realize we have learned. That is why "wild guesses" are often correct. They are, in fact, not guesses, but informed hypotheses.

Spelling applications:

- ◆ In a low-risk context, ask children to spell some of the words that they've met in their readings and on the word walls.
- ◆ Ask children to make educated guesses about the spelling of words commonly seen in the community in stores and signs.

Memory: Spatial and Rote

Our spatial memory system is universal and infinite. Motivated by "newness," our spatial memory system improves over time. Our rote memory system organizes facts and skills that require practice, both physical and mental.

We understand and remember most effectively when information and skills are embedded in a natural way. What this means is that learning is more durable when it occurs within a meaningful context of experience. This speaks for the value of field trips, investigation, demonstrations, group problem solving, communication, presentation, visuals, stories, metaphor, humor, interdisciplinary learning, and technology.

Spelling applications:

- The meaningful context of experience in spelling is, of course, reading. Encourage all kinds of reading, including comic books and cereal boxes.
- Although we pick up spelling through the visual cues of reading, we apply it in writing. Have kids design text for comic books and cereal boxes.

Challenge and Threat

Challenge enhances learning; threat inhibits learning. When a learner is challenged within her abilities, her functions are optimized. But when threatened, she retreats into a nonproductive, self-protective mode. Stress can be energizing or paralyzing. Brain researchers refer to *eustress* (good stress) and *distress* (bad stress). The amount of control that we think we have over the situation has a lot to do with our stress levels. This is why it is so important to give students choices and alternatives.

Spelling applications:

- Spelling bees (competitive spelling) are exciting only for kids who are already good at spelling. Conduct spelling bees only on a voluntary basis.
- Allow kids to select their own "challenge words."

Implications

Differentiated instruction puts students on their own and in social situations more than whole class instruction does. In DI, students take more ownership of their learning, making them, in some ways, more vulnerable than they would be in whole class instruction. While it is true that some students live in dread of being put on the spot by being "called on" when they don't know the answer, it is also true that children can distance themselves in whole class instruction, willfully disappearing as outgoing children take the ball.

A DI classroom is busy, active, full of stimuli. Distractions are all around. Every teacher has been discouraged by "groupwork" that turns into off-task socializing.

Guiding Principles of the Multiple Intelligence Paradigm

The following is adapted from *An English Teacher's Guide to Performance Tasks and Rubrics: Middle School and High School,* by Amy Benjamin, published by Eye on Education, 2000.

An understanding of Howard Gardner's theory of multiple intelligence modes can help you formulate differentiated instruction lessons designed to play into student strengths. Gardner identified the following ways of understanding the world in his book *Frames of Mind,* published in 1983.

Mark Wahl's *Math for Humans* (LivnLern Press, 1999) explains how elementary school teachers can use multiple intelligence theory to teach math. I found this interesting because so often we hear that math is a cut-and-dried subject, based only on number sense. In overviewing Gardner's eight forms of intelligence below, I've used examples for learning math.

1. Verbal-Linguistic. This is the intelligence that comes through words. Humor based on satire and wordplay are part of verbal-linguistic intelligence.
Math applications:
- Creative dramatics: Students act out skits in which the scenario has a math base—making change, telling time, measuring.
- Thinking aloud as they solve their math problems.
- Keeping math journals.
- Writing the math problem as a story.
- Learning math facts through acronyms.

2. Intrapersonal. This is the knowing of the self. Reflective pieces that call for metacognition (thinking about thinking) tap into this kind of intelligence, as do autobiographical pieces. Philosophical and spiritual thinking are also in this realm. A task that calls for knowing of the self is keeping a journal, especially a reader response journal, which asks the student to justify an opinion, react on an emotional level, or relate herself to the story.
Math applications:
- Personal reflections: Students track their learning, showing an understanding of their strengths and weaknesses and graphing their improvement.
- Developing self-understanding of math anxiety, learning to use appropriate self-talk and de-stressing techniques.
- Putting yourself in the shoes of the math problem: imagining yourself to be a multiplier or a fraction.

3. Interpersonal. This is the intelligence that involves communicating with and having insight into others. Students with this strength do well in cooperative learning groups. They make good leaders, but they also make good group members.

Math applications:
- ♦ Creative dramatics
- ♦ Math games
- ♦ Working in pairs and groups to solve math problems

4. Musical-Rhythmic. This is knowing the world through sound and rhythm. College music majors are often fine math students, and vice versa.

Math applications:
- ♦ Learn math facts through rhythm and repetition.
- ♦ Some people find that their concentration is enhanced through background music, especially classical and jazz.
- ♦ Use music to mark transitions in learning activities.
- ♦ Use music to teach counting by various intervals and to teach the tables.
- ♦ Set repetitive information to a rhythm.
- ♦ Make up jingles to remember math facts.
- ♦ Use clapping patterns to drill math facts.

5. Kinesthetic. This is knowing through physicality and performance. It is easily coupled with musical/rhythmic and creative dramatics. People with a strong kinesthetic way of understanding the world concretize an intellectual concept, such as new terminology, by acting it out.

Math applications:
- ♦ Manipulatives: playing cards, dice, cubes, Dominoes, tiles, buttons, beads, beans, blocks, ice-cream sticks, measuring instruments, colored paper, cellophane, clocks, felt, magnetic numbers
- ♦ Calculators
- ♦ Creative dramatics
- ♦ Clapping
- ♦ Games: board games, hopscotch-like games, jigsaw puzzles
- ♦ Putting things in boxes and other forms of physical organization
- ♦ Construction of physical products: scale models, geometric shapes
- ♦ Fitting things together
- ♦ Math field trips: construction sites, factories, engineering and architectural offices
- ♦ Play-action games: finding hidden treasure from a map, rescue missions, defensive strategies

6. Visual-Spatial. This is knowing the world through mental and actual pictures. We often hear people refer to themselves as *visual learners*. Such learning involves making and responding to illustrations, flow charts, symbols, and other graphic representations.

Math applications:
- ♦ Activate the "movie of the mind" when doing math: See things moving, changing, disappearing, multiplying, dividing.
- ♦ Connect pictures and designs to math (and vice versa).
- ♦ Make diagrams and flow charts to understand the steps of a procedure.

- ◆ Use color to understand part-to-whole relationships.
- ◆ Use manipulatives.
- ◆ Use concept maps.
- ◆ Encourage internal visual imagery.

7. Logical-Mathematical. This is knowing the world through patterns and numbers. We often hear the term *number person*. But these people should not be stuck memorizing rote facts just because they are good at doing so. They can also do analysis, synthesis, and applications.

Math applications:

- ◆ "What if?" questioning.
- ◆ Inductive reasoning.
- ◆ Find shortcuts.
- ◆ Work with technology and binary systems.
- ◆ Improve estimation skills in calculations and measurements.
- ◆ Improve mental math skills.
- ◆ Find other ways to do the problem to check the answer.

8. Naturalistic. This is knowing the world through nature. A strong naturalistic learner can perceive patterns and subtleties in the outdoor world. She can make predictions, gather evidence, and draw conclusions based on the complex relationships in nature. She has a keen sense of orientation and sharp observational skills.

Math applications:

- ◆ Use math tools to understand and describe the natural world.
- ◆ Math field trips: survey sites, construction sites, planetariums, science museums.
- ◆ Use natural objects as counting manipulatives.
- ◆ Use natural objects to learn about symmetry and geometric shapes.

Guiding Principles for Sensory Learning Paradigms

By *sensory learning paradigms,* we mean that individuals tend to lean toward visual, auditory, or tactile learning. You may hear this paradigm referred to as "modes of input." You will notice overlaps between this paradigm and the one for multiple intelligence. For this paradigm, we give applications for learning geography.

Visual Learning

We speak of two kinds of visual learning: *Visual/symbolic* refers to learning by looking at words; *visual/spatial* refers to learning by looking at diagrams. Geography, being about maps, is right up the alley of visual learners, but what about those who have weak visual-learning tendencies? These learners need graduated instruction in map interpretation, as well as other input modes, to understand maps.

Auditory Learning

Lucky are those who learn by hearing, for success in school is theirs. Think of how much material is delivered by oral instruction as the grades progress. A student we'll call Andrew is a weak visual learner. Geography is difficult for him. His learning specialist has taught him these strategies:

- *Self-talk.* You'll see Andrew talking out his geography homework. Saying it aloud helps him play to his strength: *OK, this is a map of New York State. I'm looking for the cities that are along the Erie Canal route. That's from Albany to Buffalo. Buffalo is up here, over near the end of the state. Albany goes straight across to the right. So the cities I'm trying to find would be right along here.*
- *Songs, jingles, slogans.* Rhythm and rhyme help Andrew to organize and remember information.
- *Partnerships.* For an auditory learner, communication with peers is a great strategy, with the added motivational benefit.
- *Recordings.* It is not practical for Andrew to record geography lessons, as there are too many inaudible comments from the class. Besides, he doesn't have the patience to relisten to an entire lesson. But there are some commercial audio-taped lessons that are sometimes appropriate.

Tactile

Tactile learners learn through their fingers. Michele, a tactile learner, learns her geography facts best by:

- Air-writing
- Jigsaw puzzles
- Writing on the board
- Making bulletin boards and displays
- Working with clay
- Putting stickers and stars on maps
- Connecting dots on maps

Guiding Principles of the Brain Laterality Paradigm

Make two fists and then put your knuckles together. That is a model of your left and right brain. The line that joins your knuckles is called the *corpus callosum*. It acts as a mediator, switchboarding between the two hemispheres. Your right side is the holistic side, the creative side. Through your right brain, you process the gist of things, as well as humor, irony, ambiguities, gray areas, and the big picture. Through your left brain, you attend to details, sequence, logical reasoning, objective facts, and orderly relationships.

It's easy to oversimplify brain laterality, thinking of some subjects as "creative" and others as "objective." Using the examples of poetry writing and math, I'll explain how both are about the whole brain.

Thinking up the ideas and imagery of poetry is a right-brain activity. Training those ideas into the pattern of rhythm and rhyme is more of a left-brain, word-engineering task. The right brain may express feelings lavishly, but it's the left brain that fits the words into a form, like tiles in a mosaic. The right brain conjures pictures and makes wild combinations of impossible things. The left brain talks sense into these words, whipping them into order. Although the right brain gets the credit, it's the left brain that manages rhyme scheme, form (sonnet, haiku, quatrain), and scansion (pattern of the beat).

As for math, we think of it as a left-brain activity, but through the right brain, we create the context of a math problem, and we give it meaning. We often describe the left brain's thinking as *linear*. The right brain is more like an interwoven network. Where the left brain makes the step-by-step calculations, the right brain does the tactical part, intuiting the holistic sense of the problem.

Intuition plays a part in all cerebral endeavors. In his book *Math for Humans*, Mark Wahl (1999) attributes intuition to the *aha!* moment of finding a pattern, that moment when it all comes together and makes sense. Although both hemispheres of the brain converge, intuition is apparently led by the right side, as the intuitive person, having processed the details (using the left brain), places them into a context (using the right brain) to formulate the flash.

You can demonstrate how brain laterality works by analyzing the clues in a mystery story. At what point does the intuitive flash occur for the mystery solver? How did the right brain put together the information that was gathered by the left brain?

In reading, the right brain extracts inferences, tone, and theme. The left brain pays attention to the details and sequence of the plot. Social subtleties and cues are picked up by the right brain. Wahl says: "Yes, intuition, movement, color, mystery, feeling, estimation, touch, and rhythm all have a place in math learning!" I have to admit that when I read this, I was surprised. My math education was about drill and practice, accuracy and precision, not some sort of feeling around for the right answer. But, being a predominantly right-brained person, I was practicing right-brained thinking all along. In fact, I didn't really "get bad" in math until, somewhere around my mid-elementary school years, I had teachers who taught math strictly through left-brained methods.

When I was in the second grade in the New York City public school system, I learned addition. Fast. (You had to do it fast, I mean. I don't think I learned it fast, although I learned it well.) Miss Kandell taught us to learn, by rote, to add our single-digit doubles: 7 + 7 = 14. That, you had to know. But, knowing that, you could add any pair of single-digit numbers by simply "upping" or "downing" by a digit or two. This, I could do. Miss Kandell would ask:

"What's 6 + 5?" You'd answer "11," and she'd say, "Why?" You'd reply: "6 + 5 is 11 because 6 + 6 is 12, minus 1 for the 5, gives you 11. And you should know your doubles." And you had to say it just that way. It worked for me.

Same with the 10s. To add, let's say, 7 + 11, you'd simply add 7 + 10 and stick on another 1, for 18. This is just pattern recognition; I learned it through playing cards, Dominoes, and the game of Jacks. Jacks was arguably the best, as you have to plan out a pattern of those pointy little metal critters before you toss the ball and grab them. Mark Wahl (1999) gives us this example of right-brain math thinking:

> Add 68 + 27 in your mind *right now. How did you get 95, the answer? Did you picture the two numbers on a kind of blackboard of the mind, add the 7 and 8, carry 1, then add the 6 and 2? Even though you were visual after a fashion (visual-symbolic), that was a fairly left-brained approach. You were reproducing the pencil and paper rules (algorithm) in your head. Or you may have rounded 68 up to 70, then added 70 + 27 = 97, then adjusted the answer downward by 2 to 95. Or your may have added the 60 and 20 part, then noted that, because of anticipated carrying, the answer would be in the 90s and end in 5, because 7 + 8 is 15. Others add 68 + 20 = 88, then add on the 7 by first adding 2 to get 90, then the other 5 to get 95. All of these routines are more right-brained because they utilize non-rule-bound relationships between parts of numbers, and because they feel or visualize patterns.*

Think about whether your teaching favors left-brain thinking. Society seems to: Traditional medicine compartmentalizes the body into "specialties"; we're accustomed to thinking of going to a specialist for the this part of the body or that, never bothering mentioning to the "east body" that we're having some tingling sensations in the "west body." Here are some ways to equalize the brain's power in traditionally right-brained subjects, like math and science:

- Give an overview of the lesson before presenting details.
- Mention the people-oriented applications of the learning.
- Ask open-ended questions.
- Turn problems into stories.
- Be humorous.
- Be metaphorical.
- Be imagistic.
- Make room for personal views, experience, background.
- Trust (or at least *acknowledge*) intuition.

Guiding Principles of Other Learning Style Paradigms

Anthony Gregorc's paradigm divides people into four categories, based on the way we approach complex thinking tasks.

1. *Concrete random.* The concrete-random thinkers in your class are the ones who think creatively, come up with alternatives, take intuitive leaps, and put together unlikely combinations. These are the kids who, when asked to make a map of the world for homework, will bring in a softball with the continents drawn on it. These are the kids who make you say, "I wouldn't have thought of that!" They need teachers who appreciate divergent thinking.

2. *Concrete sequential.* These kids love detail. They need as much structure as possible: paradigms, models, explicit directions to be followed to the letter, frameworks and timelines, deadlines and commitments. What they want from you is information, and plenty of it. Tell them what to do and how to do it, and you won't be disappointed.

3. *Abstract-sequential.* Here we have the theory lovers, the abstractionists. They are great with independent work, investigation, research, chasing ideas, philosophizing. For them, learning is not real unless they can work it through and prove it to themselves.

4. *Abstract random.* These are the communicators, the go-with-the-flow types. Guided by emotion, they like to know how the learning is a part of their lives. They learn through talking it out, so they are ideal for cooperative learning groups.

Styles and the Teacher

Now, what about you? You have a personality, a learning style, preferences and tendencies as well. You are not an adaptable information-and-skill-delivery system. Your students will mirror you, especially your emotions. My students, who tell me I'm "hyper," are pretty "hyper" themselves. I'm amazed and impressed by soft-spoken teachers whose classrooms are so much calmer than mine.

We need to remember that our tendency is to teach the way *we* learn best. It's hard to even realize this: We naturally recall how *we* learned something, and then we replicate that pedagogy. Through training, we come to understand that some children need exactly what threw us into confusion. The more you know about yourself as a learner, the more you will realize the individual nature of your own practices, and how other people may not share those practices to optimize their own learning.

Reflection

Think back to your own elementary-level schooling.

1. How did you learn a complex process, such as long division, or a large amount of information, such as the capitals of the 50 states?

2. What did your teachers do to help you comprehend and retain information?

3. What do you remember about the sensory details of the learning experience? What images have stayed with you?

Metaphors: A Paradigm for Self-Understanding

To help children clarify their roles as students in your class, ask them to compose metaphors for themselves as learners. Aristotle considered metaphor the highest form of thinking.

Mr. Hamilton introduces metaphor by bringing in an old, outdated computer. When he calls it a *dinosaur,* the children know what he means. They link a *particular* feature of the dinosaur with a *particular* feature of the computer. He's taught them metaphorical thinking.

Brilliant as metaphors are, they are all around us. They are part of our language, our very conception of the world. Metaphors lead to discovery: We understand the new in terms of the old. As such, metaphor is one of the most powerful communication tools that a teacher and a learner can have.

Some metaphors for the self (or others) are universally understood. Children know what it means to *clam up,* to *hide your head in the sand,* to be a *bully,* a *pig,* a *fish out of water.* They know that turtles and snails are associated with slowness (or self-protection through withdrawal); rabbits with speed, softness, and fear. Foxes, wolves, and chickens have metaphorical connotations that children in our culture pick up with the air they breathe. Mice are quiet and meek; rats, predatory and treacherous. These metaphors are part of our language and culture. But, in understanding themselves and their relationship to school, children need to formulate their own metaphors for themselves. Their metaphors can change, subject by subject. It's possible to be a beaver (busy and purposeful) in grammar but a little lost lamb in arithmetic. As Shakespeare said, metaphorically, "And one man in his time plays many parts" (*As You Like It,* Act II, Scene viii). Help your students understand their various roles and how they play them.

In coaxing children to think of themselves metaphorically, avoid words that would reinforce a negative image, especially those associated with "dumbness," such as *ox.* An emergent learner can think of herself as a caterpillar or a budding flower. Such images have the power to imbue the learner with patience, self-care, hope. The right metaphor can help a child feel in control.

Explore other metaphorical fields with children: plant life, machinery, tools, and office supplies. Any field that has variety, and objects that can change or be put to use, is fertile for claiming the metaphorical self. Try modes of transportation, weather and other natural phenomena, sports and sports equipment.

Children can get a sense of their own preciousness through metaphor. Consider this extended metaphor from *Bridging: A Teacher's Guide to Metaphorical Thinking* (Pugh et al., 1992):

> *Through metaphor, one may devise what we can call an emotional philosophy of life. At its beginning, life is like a delicate vase, so perfect as to be translucent but also extremely fragile, whereas the determination to*

survive must be like cement. When life gets broken, as it inevitably does, one must rebuild it with emotional cement. The object loses its original perfection, yet it becomes stronger each time the breaking-and-mending process occurs. In time, the object may have been mended so many times that it becomes almost all cement, yet in tiny places where the original material shines through, one sees anew the beauty of the object. In the end it is the design, and not the material, that matters. What we attain through living is our own constructive activity with our lives, not an original endowment.

Here is a lesson that leads children to understand themselves metaphorically:

1. Select a category, such as "things you can buy at Staples" or "plants." Make a list of 20 items that fit into the category.
2. For each item, determine if you think it is "positive" or "negative" for *you.*
3. Make two columns: *Me* and *Not Me.*
    - Sort the items into those that are you and those that are not you.
    - To expand this activity:
    Explain why the items in the *Me* column represent you.

Add another column for *Wanna Be Me,* and explain what you would have to do to get those items into the *Me* column.

And you? What's your metaphor for yourself as a teacher? Are you pulling teeth? Are you a scout, leading an expedition through a trail that you've blazed before, but that still holds surprises and wonder for you? Are you a museum guide, showing off the treasures of civilization? Are you a newspaper, full of information for getting along in today's world? Are you a worksite foreman, answerable to the higher-ups for the production level of your unit? Are you Inspector 19 at the underwear-making factory? An emcee or party host? What would be the most productive and rewarding metaphor that you could conceive for yourself as an educator? What are the qualities of this model? How far away are you from this ideal? How can you get there?

All of this has relevance to DI, because DI is about nothing if not distinguishing and defining the individual. Metaphor-making for the self does distinguish and define the self through a combination of self-reflection, self-imaging, and goal setting.

Reflection:
Classroom Metaphors

What are the positive and negative implications of the following metaphors for a classroom or a school? How close is your situation to these? How can you change that?

1. Ant farm
2. Corporate boardroom
3. Garden

4. Family
5. Cruise ship
6. Factory

Puppets, Masques, and Make-Up as a Paradigm for Differentiated Instruction

The puppet, an ancient visual metaphor, is a powerful learning paradigm, representing real life, but with a lot more expressive freedom. The therapeutic use of puppets is well known. Here, we will look at some ways that teachers can use puppets as a tool for differentiating instruction.

Every puppet has its own persona, created both by the designer of the puppet and by the puppeteer. Through this persona, the child can ask questions and make comments attributed to the character, not to the child. Any object can become a puppet: All it needs is a voice. Through that voice, children can make great strides in their use of language, not only in vocabulary but also in dialect, register (degree of formality in speech), and subject matter.

I've used puppets to teach metacognition in reading and math. "Mr. MetaReader" is a puppet that watches over me as I read. Mr. MetaReader and I model effective reading strategies. He makes sure that I understand, slapping me awake when I'm drifting, reminding me to reread what I don't understand, helping me summon background information on the topic before "we" begin reading. Mr. MetaReader tells me not to get discouraged when I run into words I don't know: *Just try to get the gist, try to figure out the new word from the cues in the sentence. See if you already know part of that word, and, if all else fails, ask someone what the word means, or look it up in the glossary or a dictionary.* Then Mr. MetaReader helps me refocus on the reading task: *Now, where were we?*

Puppets play into so many of the learning channels: visual, auditor, tactile, kinesthetic, interpersonal, intrapersonal. They help children speak in public, speak in a foreign language, try out new words, be more clownish than they would dare to be "on their own." They can enact historical situations, playing out the power relationships between royalty and subject, lord and serf. Puppets can turn stories into plays, science experiments into skits, math problems into interactions between opposing forces. Teachers can use puppets to communicate with English language learners. They can remind us, as Mr. MetaReader does, of the mental habits we need to internalize.

Summary

This chapter has offered paradigms through which differentiated instruction can be established based on *how* different people learn best. They are not mutually exclusive They blend together in an active classroom where teachers make decisions about the kids in front of them. Although the paradigms describe various ways of learning, they are united by the guiding principles that learning is an active, ongoing process requiring physical, emotional, and intellectual investment on the part of the learner as well as the teacher.

In all of these paradigms, children learn best, and retain what they've learned, when they feel safe, use what they already know, self-monitor, and build up learning capacity by multisensory input.

11

Model Differentiated Instruction Lessons

Mrs. Leighton's State Capitals Project: Fifth Grade

Mrs. Leighton teaches fifth grade. She wants her students to know the capitals of the 50 states. She has an intuitive sense of the importance of this knowledge: tradition, general information about our country, the intrinsic value of memorizing 50 pieces of information. Having used mnemonics, visuals, kinesthetics, all kinds of worksheets, games, puzzles, and gimmicks, she recognized that these methods were not elevating the task beyond a literal level.

As for differentiation, Mrs. Leighton didn't want to differentiate the content: She wanted everyone in the class to know the 50 capitals. She didn't want to differentiate the assessment, either: Everyone had to name the 50 capitals. Although this learning experience may seem too rigid for differentiation, a little divergent thinking yielded a richer engagement.

Mrs. Leighton decided to have her students learn the capitals by examining some implications of geography. Why would a particular city be chosen over another, often larger and more bustling, as the capital? She divided her 28 children into even groups of four.

First, she asked the groups to consider all the different ways that the 50 states could be divided: by region, alphabetically, by geographical features (mountain states, plains states, desert states), by population density, by the number of large cities, and by size. Each group proposed a division scheme that they thought made the most sense, and they explained their reasoning to the class. The class voted that they would divide the states by geographical region, the reason being that they thought they could learn the states best that way.

With each of the seven groups having a block of seven states to work with (and one group having eight), the next step was to figure out why the capitals were what they were. So each group had to consider these questions:

1. What kinds of things need to happen in a state capital?

2. Where would be the best place to locate a state capital so that these things can be done?

3. What happens to a city and its suburbs once it becomes the state capital?

4. If you were to pick out a capital city for a state, what would be three factors that you would consider? Put these factors in order of importance.

Thus, the learning of state capitals became a problem-solving activity, one that integrated knowledge of geography, population patterns, government, economics, and other social studies concepts.

Performance Tasks for the State Capitals Project

Mrs. Leighton gave each student a choice of one of the following ways to show what they know about state capitals. Students had to choose five states each, from different regions.

- ◆ Pretending that you are a particular state capital, write a letter to the people of your state proposing yourself as the state capital. You may give one good reason, or several. In your letter, explain why you are a better choice than two other major cities in your state.

- ◆ Draw or trace a map of the state, indicating where the state capital is and what the key geographical features of the state are. In the margins, list several reasons why the state capital is located in this place.

- ◆ Find five state capitals that have something in common, such as being near a river, having easy access, being in a central location. Make a circle in the center of your page, and write the common feature in the circle. Write the capitals (and their states) on the radii of the circle.

- ◆ With a partner, play out a skit in which representatives from two cities of a state argue their points for having their city as the state capital.

- ◆ Design a postage stamp for a particular state capital. Your stamp should represent key features of both the city and its state.

- ◆ Design a travel brochure for a particular state capital. Like the postage stamp, your travel brochure should represent key features of both the city and the state.

In addition to the performance task, students still had to take the traditional fill-in test on the 50 state capitals. So they still had to work on their memorization skills. However, with the higher-level learning involved in the capitals project, memorization was fortified and informed by real associations. We have all kinds of effective tricks for memorization, and memorization is important. But memorization without reasoning tends to fade.

A variation of Mrs. Leighton's state capitals project is to set up learning stations for the given number of regions and have traveling groups of students visiting each station, answering the essential questions for each.

Another variation on a higher level of thinking is to have students solve the following hypothetical problem:

For economic reasons, the United States Congress has decided that instead of having 50 states, we should have 25. Every state will have to unify with another state. The states may be contiguous (next to each other) or not contiguous, depending on your plan:

1. Consider the advantages and disadvantages of this idea.

2. Propose a new organization plan for the 50 states, consisting of 25 states. For each pair, write your reason for joining the two states. In some case, you may decide to join three or four states together, leaving other states the way they are. You must end up with 25 states.

3. For each newly formed state, you must designate one capital. That capital can be one of the existing ones, or you may propose a brand-new location as the capital.

In doing this project, Mrs. Leighton's students reinforced their familiarity with American geography. They also learned why borders are where they are and how state government works. They developed a keener sense of what regions in this United States are all about: where the unofficial cultural dividing lines are, social characteristics of regions, ethnic composition, economic conditions.

Mrs. Leighton's state capital project is differentiated instruction because the reasoning, solutions, and proposals are expected to vary from group to group and because each student in the group would be expected to contribute his or her own knowledge to the problem-solving process.

Ms. Collins' Second Grade Reading Lesson

Janice Collins teaches second grade. Her number 1 priority is to get her second graders up to grade level, at least, in reading. Aware that reading skills are the foundation for most school-based learning, Janice has achieved success with her students by having them work in groups in a DI structure. The lesson plan presented here is part of the Language Arts curriculum. Janice begins the planning process by spending many hours previewing new reading/language materials.

It is month 6 in the second grade. Janice has 14 students in her class: Four are below grade level by approximately half a year, but they have advanced by a full year so far in Janice's class. Janice has worked hard with these children on phonics, and their work has indeed paid off in significant, measurable growth. Three students test out as just a couple of months behind, and three test out at a good year ahead. The remaining four are at grade level.

First, she pretests her second graders for reading, using three instruments: a placement test by Ginn, a sight-word list (Dolche), and something called a *running record*, which consists of short, multileveled passages in which all reading errors are recorded and evaluated, along with comprehension questions. Another test that Janice considers is the *Renaissance Reading®* computer program, which has students reading on their own independent level and then answering phonics and comprehension questions, also on the computer. From these instruments, Janice derives a tentative profile of her students' reading needs.

Janice's interest inventory reveals that all of her children are interested in animals. So she has lots of reading material about all creatures great and small. Students choose their reading material from a collection of diverse readings about animals, at various levels and subtopics. She has several activity centers, each based on a specific objective. As the children select, read, and follow-up with activities, Janice observes carefully and jots down notes.

A Differentiated Instruction Lesson Plan for Reading in the Second Grade

Objectives:

- The student will be aware from reading a story what is meant by *cause and effect*. She will be able to tell about a cause and effect that occurs in a given story.
- The student will be able to identify words with the *ow/ow* sounds and identify the sounds in her reading, writing, and speech.

Materials:

- Various books at different reading levels:

  Below Level: *Never Bored on the Farm, The County Park, Wilbur the Hound, Howard the Twin, What the Clown Sees* (Harcourt). These books feature the *ou/ow* sound.

  On-Level: *Howie's Baby Boa.*

  Above Level: *All About Snakes.*

- Various other books and reading materials available for independent-choice reading:

  Berenstain Bears, Hedgehog, Harry and Mudge, nonfiction selections

- Various skill sheets.
- Writing materials: crayons, markers, paper, construction paper, recipe cards, cubes.

Setup

- The room is set up with learning centers: readings, activities, assessment.

Activities

- Whole class: KWL chart on cause and effect; review of the concept; establishment of expectations for the upcoming learning experience.
- Groups: Before the students break into groups, diverging toward various centers, Janice clarifies what they are to be looking for in the story: cause/effect and the *ou/ow* sound.

The independent readers read *All About Snakes,* while the on-grade-level readers form partnerships to read *The Day Jimmy's Boa Ate the Wash.* Janice needs to give the below-level group intensive phonics instruction. After they review the relevant phonics, these children follow a familiar procedure of recording their oral reading on a tape recorder. Students needing extra practice on the *ou/ow* sound can use a computer program that addresses many phonics skills. There are also comprehension computer programs available for cause and effect.

◆ Now, the centers: When the groups finish their assigned reading, they go to one of two main centers: cause and effect and *ou/ow* mastery. Each center has different activities based on the skill level, working toward mastery of the objectives.

◆ The cause and effect center looks like this: Heterogeneous groups of kids work on different skills, using construction paper, writing materials, and skill sheets at different levels. For example, the students who need the most basic work have a skill sheet that has several short passages with a single cause and effect that is clearly stated. The next group up reads a longer passage having several causes and effects implied. The top level writes a short story with at least six sentences in which there is at least one cause and effect relationship. They will share it with a classmate, asking the classmate to identify the cause and effect. Then, to unify the class, each child makes a cover for her work, illustrating one cause and effect relationship from her reading.

Evaluation and assessment: Janice bases her judgments on the quality of the work completed at the center. Janice likes to use the skill worksheets provided by the publisher of her reading series. She says, "Let the professionals help me out in doing this kind of work. Plus, they make the work more interesting and artful."

◆ Now, the *ou/ow* center on the other side of the room: Janice has set up three cubing tasks. The children are required to finish three of the sides of their cube and put their written work into their work folders. This is a classroom management system that Janice's students are used to.

CUBE RED:

Note: The children have their books with them.

a. Write five words from your reading that have the *ou/ow* sound. Spell them correctly.

b. Use two *ou/ow* words in a sentence. You may record your sentence or write it.

c. Do the RED skill sheet on *ou/ow* words. [These sheets consist of sentence construction exercises that go along with pictures that represent the reading.]

d. On recipe cards, write four *ou/ow* words, and use them in sentences on paper, on the recorder, or with the teacher.

e. Fill in the RED paragraph worksheet with words from the *ou/ow* word wall.

f. Illustrate an action *ou/ow* would take, and write a caption.

CUBE BLUE:

a. Use four *ou/ow* words in a paragraph. Write at least four sentences.

b. Do the BLUE skill sheet on *ou/ow* words.

c. Write and illustrate a paragraph about the main character in your book. Use at least four *ou/ow* words. Underline them.

d. Write a one-sentence detail about the setting of your story. Use two *ou/ow* words.

e. Do the BUE paragraph worksheet with words from the *ou/ow* word wall.

f. Illustrate your favorite part of the story. Use *ou/ow* words in a written description of your illustration.

CUBE GREEN:

a. Write a short story using at least 10 *ou/ow* words. Use at least six sentences, and draw an illustration. Share it with classmates.

b. Do the GREEN skill sheet.

c. Describe two main characters in your book. Write three sentences about each character. Use the dictionary, and write at least four *ou/ow* words to describe the characters.

d. Make a word web using an *ou/ow* word as the base. Use at least three other *ou/ow* words in your web.

e. Write a moral to your story. Use three *ou/ow* words.

f. Make a storyboard for your story. Use at least three cells. Write captions, using at least four *ou/ow* words.

Teacher Reflection: *So How Did It Go?*

Janice gives the following assessment of the lesson:

This was a very interesting learning experience for both me and my students! For one thing, I wanted to do the lesson before spring break, so I kind of hurried into presenting the lesson. My students are fairly used to different grouping techniques, but, even so, they were not ready for the independence that I was expecting of them in doing the cubing tasks. They often read books on a central theme at different levels, and they often do some differentiated center skill work. But they were totally unprepared for the cubing tasks at this point!

As I mentioned, I have four lower-level readers, seven mid-range, and three above-average. Even the higher-level readers had difficulty coping with the cubing tasks.

First of all, you have to understand (and sometimes even I have to understand) that second graders are still VERY primary. They really require step-by-step instruction and practice before they can be expected to accomplish routines/directions/skills on their own. This is true of the cubing strategy. I think that we would have to take this very slowly throughout the year, practicing at first with group with a cubing activity several times. Again, a step-by-step procedure, practicing several times, would be required for kids at second grade to be able to do this independently—and only then if the instructions on the cubes were pretty rote and easy to understand at first—giving way to more complex instructions slowly. I had so many kids who were continually asking how they should proceed. It was quite confusing this first time, and my expectations were way too broad and complicated without having first gone through the procedure in practice. Second graders need to be able to build upon their instructional skills as well as their reading skills, and I didn't allow them the time nor the practice TO DO THIS.

I do feel that by this time next year, however, I may be able to use such a lesson plan, if we proceed slowly throughout the year to this point. A few students were able to accomplish some of the tasks on their own. When I sat down with each student and went over the instructions on each cube individually, they were able to put it together and come up with the required tasks. They were just not ready to go off on their own with this yet.

After we worked one-on-one for a while, I was able to assess that each student had mastered the two concepts we were working on—at least on the most basic level. It was a successful lesson, built upon other lessons on the same topic, though. Second graders usually need repetition on different levels before mastery.

My students did think the outcome was beneficial, and the "assignments" were fun—especially in the area of having choice. I really didn't have any students complaining about "fairness" in their work or in my expectations of their work. For one thing, we have talked and talked about this during other group lessons. For another, they were way too busy trying to cope with some of the confusion that was going on at the time!

In looking back, I have to laugh at my foibles in this lesson. I am excited about differentiated learning and about implementing it into my lessons. But I realize, too, that I must progress more slowly, build it up with the kids, and use it carefully.

The comprehension section of the lesson went rather smoothly. However, the class is much more familiar with the few choices that I had available at the centers—most often in science, though. They were able to accomplish the required tasks, and I was able to evaluate their work much more on an individual basis in this area.

This lesson was as much a learning experience for me as for my students. While we did not accomplish all that I had wished we would, I now know how to proceed from here, that is, to start much more slowly and to build our knowledge of differentiated learning lessons as well as the skills we're working to master. A very valuable learning experience!

What We Can Learn from Janice

What we've seen here is a slice of life from a savvy, experienced teacher. Janice took a risk, as anyone does who ventures into a new teaching strategy. Her planning was intuitive and informed, and her class seemed ready to make the jump based on their classroom training and some routines that would seem to flow into the learning center model. Janice found out that she needed to plan even more carefully and prepare the students better than she had thought—and she did think and plan quite a lot.

Let's look at what Janice did right: She had a goal, and her goal fit into the context of what she had been working with the kids on all year—reading improvement in specific areas. She preassessed, using a variety of proven instruments. She did a great job of laying out the task for the children and framing the DI work with whole class instruction before and after. And, most importantly, she reflected so that she could adjust her teaching for next time. In her reflective comments, she maintains optimism, a sense of humor about herself, and renewed determination. We can all be impressed by the way Janice works *with* the children, carefully observing them with her own improvement as a teacher in mind. She recognizes what went a little haywire. She doesn't blame herself. She doesn't blame the children. She simply realizes what has to be done to make differentiated instruction viable.

The problems that Janice ran into are about classroom management. It's very difficult to foresee how all the moving parts of a classroom (namely, children) are going to disperse themselves once you turn them loose. Janice's resolve is to integrate DI protocols more systematically in future classes.

Janice's model here could also be applied to math instruction: establish objectives, preassess, divide the class into three tiers, assign math tasks for each tier, and conduct a whole class lesson beginning with KWL and clarifying the content. Set up two main activity centers where the children advance their skills. Bring the lesson back to whole class instruction, encouraging lots of student talk and sharing new knowledge.

Skilled teachers aren't born that way. They become that way by doing what Janice has done: having a plan and entering cautiously into a new paradigm, then riding over the rough spots, perhaps being overwhelmed but having the good nature to plow through anyway, making mental and written notes about how it can be done better next time.

The Story of the First Graders and the Buttons

The purpose of the button lesson is to teach children how to categorize and find patterns. This is an interdisciplinary lesson: Math, language arts, science, and social studies skills are being practiced. In all classes, students must find differences and similarities, name groups, regroup things, find patterns.

Children can do the button activity individually, in pairs, or as groups. Children are divided into groups based on their social and emotional maturity. Those needing the most teacher intervention will have the largest buttons that are also the fewest in number and the least subtle in differences. Those who the teacher thinks can function on the highest level in the class have smaller buttons and more of them, and the buttons will be more subtle in their variety.

The idea is to group by various categories: size, color, shape, number of holes, and material. Each student writes or says a sentence to describe her reason for placing the buttons in the particular grouping. The teacher brings the students back together as a class to create a graph of all the different groupings created.

Other Ways to Use Buttons to Teach Math and Language Arts in the Primary Grades

- ◆ Create and name patterns with the buttons.
- ◆ Estimate the number of buttons in a container.
- ◆ Make "even" and "uneven" piles of buttons.
- ◆ Show that two piles with equal numbers can be different sizes if the sizes of the buttons themselves are different.
- ◆ Weigh and measure the buttons.
- ◆ Have students look at a pattern of buttons and then close their eyes while one button is taken away. Then ask them to say which one was taken away.
- ◆ Play the "Guess My Button" game: Similar to "Twenty Questions," children ask questions to narrow the field to a particular button.
- ◆ Understand the metaphorical meaning of the word *button*: elevator buttons, buttons on websites, car-lock buttons, alarm-clock buttons, buttons with messages.
- ◆ Notice how buttons are used to represent eyes on stuffed animals: What are the similarities between eyes and buttons?
- ◆ Practice fine motor skills and hand-eye coordination by stringing buttons.
- ◆ Match buttons to their twins.
- ◆ Judge the predominant color in a jar of buttons.
- ◆ Match buttons to buttonholes.
- ◆ Use words to explain how to close a button.

Dawn Alcera's Reading in Science Lessons

Dawn Alcera is a special education teacher in Putnam Valley Elementary School in New York:

> For many students, reading science text is like reading another language. Sure, they can decode most of the words on the page, but they can't derive meaning from them. Especially my special education students. They need to become familiar with the patterns of science language and with strategies for making the unfamiliar more familiar. Helping them do so is my job. This year, in addition to the strategies that I already use with them (SQ3R, reciprocal teaching, outlining and webbing), I tried out three that I recently read about:
>
> ♦ Listening to science materials being read aloud
>
> ♦ Interpreting the structure of science text in terms of characters, plot and setting
>
> ♦ Socializing in science through conversation circles.
>
> Reading fiction tends to be easier than reading nonfiction because readers are familiar with the conventions of fictional writing: They know how to identify the character, plot, and setting. They've been taught to make predictions while they read. They visualize, putting themselves into the story. If they can do this, it's because they've heard fiction and poetry read to them by teachers and parents.. But how many teachers and parents have read science passages aloud to children?. Student are not used to listening to science language being read to them, and they are not comfortable reading it themselves.
>
> Before students can effectively read science text, they need to become familiar with its structure. To do this, I tried opening my science lessons each day by "reading science" aloud. I read a few paragraphs of interesting material based on the current topic. I found some of the material from the textbook, and some from newspaper or magazine articles. I read aloud for three to five minutes, stopping in the middle of a sentence. Then, I'd leave the article available to any student interested in further examination. The read-alouds familiarized students with science language: syntax, organization, and vocabulary.
>
> I've begun animating science by presenting it in literary terms: plot, characters, setting. I paired up students to read a piece of science text and then decide what elements of the text could be the characters, setting, and plot. Let's say they read a section on photosynthesis. Possible characters could be the sun, oxygen, carbon dioxide, and chlorophyll. The process of photosynthesis is the plot; the plant is the setting. This schema builds on prior knowledge of how things work.

Socialization. I know the value of allowing students to interact and verbalize what they have learned. I've applied the structure of literary circles to science learning. I place the students in groups of four and assign them each a role: question maker, reader, predictor, and summarizer. The role is written on index cards (to provide a visual and tactile piece for my students with learning challenges). The students read an assigned section of the text and carry out their assigned roles. Then, they pass the cards clockwise and read the next section; now, they have new roles. They continue this rotation until the reading is completed. I find that the students enjoy interacting with each other and benefit from listening to each other read, predict, answer questions, and summarize. After this, they create an outline or web to review the material and make it their own. I want them to apply the reading skills that they learned in class to their independent reading. For homework, they read a section of a chapter, write down questions, make predictions, and answer their own questions. This procedure can be used for all levels of students: advanced students can comprehend challenging material in this way.

Making science reading more informed by literary reading has led to big improvements in my students' interest in and comprehension of science. It is more exciting and engaging than the dusty old practice of assigning readings and simply requiring students to answer the questions at the end of the chapters. All that does is get the students to mechanically scan for the answers. That way, they read without context or involvement: reading for information, but not understanding. To read for understanding in science, readers need to activate prior knowledge, animate the text, and have multiple opportunities to learn the information.

Using Creative Dramatics and Visualization to Teach Math

Background

Mark Wahl, author of *Math for Humans* (1999), teaches math in a uniquely creative way. He animates numbers. Here's what it looks like:

Mathematical symbols, such as numbers and operations, become characters in a drama. Negative numbers are the bad guys; positives, the good guys. Powers become forces that generate just that: power. The problem to be solved becomes an episode in which there is a conflict. Think of it like this: (–8) is a bad guy, but when he clashes with (+19), we're going to end up with the good guy winning. We're still on the good guy side when we add these numbers together.

It gets better. Wahl conceives of two different "lands": The Land of Multiplication and the Land of Addition. In the Land of Multiplication, multiplication, of course, goes on, but you have other stuff, like powers and square roots, happening. But in the Land of Addition, there's only enough air supply for addition and subtraction. In the Land of Addition, Zero means, well, nothing. It can go up to any number and not even be noticed. Zero is Nobody in the Land of Addition. Now, you put Zero in the Land of Multiplication, and it's a killer. Next, take One. One is the Nobody of the Land of Multiplication, but it does have an effect, if gentle, in the Land of Addition.

We go on. Consider: [any number] to the zero power. What that means is that there are no factors multiplying that number. Nothing is happening. What's Nothing in the Land of Multiplication? Well, it's One. A number to the zero power yields One. So the signifier of zero power would be One. This is not to be confused with what would happen in the Land of Addition, where One means that something is happening. But, remember, powers do not exist in the Land of Addition—only in the Land of Multiplication.

You or I may not need this. Wahl's Imaginary Number Land may, in fact, confuse us. But it may work magic for some kids who do well with stories and imagery. Math is about conflict, clashes, compromises. These are the elements of drama.

Appendix A
Assessment Guide

Intellectual	Social	Emotional
How the child integrates new information	*How the child interacts with peers and adults*	*How the child acts when told "no"*
Considerations:	*Considerations:*	*Considerations:*
◆ Makes connections ◆ Organizes information ◆ Practices and perseveres ◆ Uses new words well ◆ Reasons well ◆ Can memorize ◆ Expresses ideas ◆ Uses accurate language ◆ Uses a variety of strategies ◆ Adapts and adjusts ◆ Retains information ◆ Has age-appropriate study skills	◆ Communicates needs ◆ Makes eye contact ◆ Reads others' needs ◆ Is gregarious ◆ Is liked by others ◆ Shares possessions ◆ Shows empathy and kindness ◆ Is appropriately private ◆ Reads social signals ◆ Participates in group situations ◆ Has age-appropriate friends	◆ Can defer personal needs ◆ Can express frustration in words ◆ Can control aggressiveness ◆ Accepts authority ◆ Is resilient ◆ Accepts change ◆ Is appropriately remorseful ◆ Learns from mistakes ◆ Is reasonably happy ◆ Has age-appropriate impulsivity control

Appendix B
Teaching Emotionally Fragile Children

- Use concrete language.
- Give clear, consistent directions.
- Establish routine and expectations.
- Use lots of visual supports.
- Give either a visual or an auditory task. Avoid giving both at the same time.
- Explain what is going to happen next.
- Don't expect kids to generalize or extrapolate easily. Don't expect them to "learn from their mistakes" easily, especially when the "mistakes" result from an emotional deficit, such as impulsivity.
- Use lots of refrains and slogans as behavioral reminders.
- Avoid wordy explanations.
- Give immediate feedback.
- Use redirection to stop a behavior, rather than harsh *no* words.
- Place the child's desk near good role models, if the child will not distract them.
- Emphasize the child's strengths and interests.
- Lead up to transitions.
- Match spelling words to a picture or photograph of the item.
- Be as predictable and structured as possible.
- Encourage positive socialization.
- Understand that what you think are clear, nonverbal cues and facial expressions may not work.
- Celebrate small victories.

Appendix C

Teaching Gifted and Talented Children

- Encourage and model divergent thinking.
- Encourage and model metaphorical thinking.
- Encourage and model abstract thinking.
- Encourage and model extrapolations.
- Remember that although bright children often have superior communication skills and maturity, these qualities do not necessarily go together.
- Speak with elevated language.
- Develop in the child a sense of leadership without a sense of superiority.
- Offer opportunities for flexible thinking.
- Offer opportunities for thinking about ambiguities, nuances, and subtleties.
- Offer opportunities for independent work.
- Avoid putting bright students "on hold" while others catch up or are remediated.
- Avoid the appearance and the reality of using bright students to teach others at no advantage to themselves.
- Enhance curricula through depth and complexity, rather than just increasing the quantity. Avoid the appearance or reality of having brighter kids just doing more of the same.
- Stress interdisciplinary connections.
- Stress the arts.
- Stress practical application of abstract concepts.
- Offer opportunities to learn another language.
- Offer opportunities for successful students to explain to peers how they went about doing a multistep task.
- Offer opportunities for successful students to plan and reflect upon their own learning in terms of goals and accomplishments.

- Stress self-monitoring and self-correcting habits.
- Encourage and model transcendence of the obvious.
- Encourage and model multitasking.
- Encourage and model attention to detail.
- Encourage and model story-telling as a means of communicating information.

Appendix D
Planning Differentiated Instruction

Topic:

Standards:

Essential Questions:

What do I want to differentiate?

The content (what students learn)

The process (how students learn)

The product (how students show what they know)

Appendix E

A Mental Map for the Differentiated Instruction Teacher

Where am I going?
How will I get there?
How will I know when I've arrived?

1. What do I want students to know and be able to do as a result of this lesson (or lesson series)?
2. Will differentiating instruction improve learning?
3. Do I want to differentiate for content, process, or assessment, or a combination of the three?
4. Do I need to preassess?
5. How will I group the students?
6. How will I manage the learning conditions of the class (moving students around, balancing the need for communication versus the need for quiet, assessing the need for resources)?
7. Will I be using resources such as the library and the computer lab?
8. What is my time frame? What will students do if they finish early?
9. Will all students be doing critical thinking?
10. Will everyone be graded using the same criteria? Do I need a rubric?
11. How will I communicate with the students while they are working?
12. Do I have a plan for students who fall significantly behind in their work?
13. Will absences (of students or myself) interfere significantly with the progress of a group or pair?
14. Does this work meet the Standards in at least one subject area?
15. Am I differentiating instruction because I believe that students will learn more than they would by traditional whole class instruction?
16. How does this DI work fall into the learning theory that new information must be integrated with known information?
17. Is this DI work a language-rich experience?

18. Which of the following applies to this DI work?
    - communication
    - creativity
    - critical thinking
    - detail work
    - interdisciplinary learning
    - logic
    - metacognition
    - modulated levels of depth and complexity
    - point of view
    - putting new information to work
    - student choice
    - time management

Appendix F

The Think Test

We want children to do higher-level thinking, to put ideas together and take them apart, to transcend the obvious. This list will facilitate your evaluation of the learning tasks that you assign to students. It will help you know when you are asking students to think critically.

- Subject:
  - General:
  - Specific:
- Describe the learning experience. What will the students be doing? Hearing? Reading? Saying? Seeing?
- Which, if any, of the following critical thinking skills apply to this learning experience?
  - Discerning similarities between unlike things
  - Discerning differences between like things
  - Evaluating something against criteria
  - Establishing criteria
  - Justifying an assertion
  - Sorting, classifying, categorizing
  - Applying new words
  - Interdisciplinary synthesis (putting ideas from different subjects together)
  - Understanding part-to-whole relationships
  - Linking new information to known information
  - Applying a reading strategy
  - Communicating with peers
  - Communicating with adults
  - Formulating hypotheses
  - Formulating questions
  - Using complex sentence structure in speech or writing
  - Using language in a more formal register than that used in ordinary conversation
  - Multitasking

- Using technology
- Deferring judgment until all the facts are in:
- Making judgments about the value or applicability of one thing over another (making informed choices)
- Relating academic material to the world outside of school
- Thinking introspectively
- Negotiating with others
- Distinguishing fact from opinion
- Making inferences
- Being flexible as to the meaning of words in context
- Learning through trial and error
- Understanding the "why" of things
- Moving from one genre to another
- Locating information
- Going from general to specific, and back to general
- Tolerating ambiguity
- Distinguishing emotion from reason
- Integrating emotion with reason
- Understanding procedures, protocols, conventions, sequence, process

Appendix G

Here's Where You Lose Me, Teacher

You lose me when you use big words.

You lose me when you draw diagrams.

You lose me when you don't give examples.

You lose me when I'm hearing too many numbers.

You lose me when you aren't there and I have to work on my own.

You lose me when we have class in a different place.

You lose me when you are in a grouchy mood.

You lose me when I am in a grouchy mood.

You lose me after lunch.

You lose me before lunch.

You lose me when everybody's talking.

You lose me when you show maps.

You lose me when I'm afraid you will call on me.

You lose me when you say something is going to be hard.

You lose me when you say something is going to be easy (and it isn't).

You lose me when you talk about current events.

You lose me when you don't write important things on the board.

You lose me when you change what you say.

You lose me when you don't look my way.

You lose me when you talk too fast.

You lose me when you talk too slow.

You lose me when _____.

Appendix H

The State-of-the-Art Differentiated Instruction Classroom

If you could design a "gourmet classroom," it might look like this:

- It would be equipped with: overhead projector, data/video projection system supporting computer graphics and text, DVD player and display screen, multiple network ports for the Internet, mobile carts for AV equipment, mounted wide-screen television projection system, laptops.

- It would have a quiet reading area with audio equipment and headphones, in-class library and student book exchange center, learning center for manipulatives, time-out space, teacher conferencing space, white board sliders.

- There would be plenty of bulletin board space, shelves, cubbies, art supplies of all kinds, demonstration clocks, and an erasable handwriting chart that kids could overwrite on.

- Of course, you'd have a science center with copious plants and little furry animals (with food), weights and measures, rocks and minerals, all kinds of take-apart and put-together machines, and weather-reading devices.

- And . . . there would be a telephone with an outside connection (but *no* intercom!).

Appendix I

Responding to Wrong Answers

One of the most difficult communication challenges for a teacher is to tell a student that she is wrong without embarrassing or discouraging her.

Responding with "I" Statements

♦ Tell me more. [*Sometimes, when students elaborate, they say something you can redirect.*]
♦ I'm trying to understand what you're thinking.
♦ Tell me why.
♦ I didn't look at it that way. Can you explain that for me?
♦ Help me understand you.
♦ I'm thinking about what you're saying. [*Pause for elaboration.*]
♦ I may not be making myself clear to you. Let me try again.

Responding with "But . . . " Statements

♦ I think I know how you're looking at this: You're thinking . . . , but . . .
♦ A lot of people think that, but . . .
♦ That's the tricky part, but . . .
♦ That would be true if. . . . , but . . .

Responding with Redirection

♦ Think about what we said about . . .
♦ Think about what . . . means.
♦ Go back to the beginning of the story . . .
♦ Take another look at the ending . . .
♦ How many . . . do we have?
♦ Try doing this: . . .

Your Internal Response

Your students will learn better if you approach their wrong answers analytically: What are they thinking? How can you help?

- Are they operating under the wrong premise?
- Are they confusing one term with another?
- Are they using ineffective shortcuts?
- Are they misapplying a rule?
- Are they misunderstanding the nature of the question?
- Are they missing chunks of information due to absence when the rest of the class learned something?
- Are they having trouble recovering from a learning lapse, such as a vacation, snow day, field trip, or other break in the routine?
- Are they emotionally distressed for family reasons? General societal reasons? Health, nutrition, or sleeplessness reasons? Are they upset with other children in the class? Are they upset with you?
- Do they need to be evaluated by a learning specialist?
- Has their logic gone astray?
- Do they understand your language?
- Are there physical distractions, such as hall noise, classroom noise, construction, excessive heat or cold?

Adjustments

You can't adjust for all of the above for all students. But you may be able to do the following:

- Rephrase the question: Simplify your language by defining academic terminology in a more cue-laden context.
- Slow the pace.
- Build-in review and reinforcement.
- Provide more visuals and multisensory cues.
- Connect to background knowledge.
- Lighten up the tone in the room.
- Be more concrete: Give examples.
- Teach sitting down, eye-to-eye with the children.
- Provide additional supports from the various resources available.
- Think diagnostically and scientifically, *and, at the same time . . .*
- Think intuitively and holistically.
- Ask yourself if you are teaching the way you learn, rather than the way some of your students learn.

- Conceptualize a scale of 1 to 10, in which your instruction may be on level 8, and a student's comprehension is on level 4. Think of how you can communicate at level 5, then 6, then 7, then 8 with that student.
- Don't give up!

Author's Note

If you are not afraid to admit your own lack of knowledge about some things, if you admit being wrong sometimes, you will foster an environment in which students are freer to do the same. Never preside over an environment in which children or adults feel that giving a wrong answer means losing face. On the other hand, don't be mealy-mouthed or equivocal when children are wrong in their answers or behavior.

Appendix J

Scaffolding and Differentiated Instruction

Scaffolding refers to the supports and structures that teachers provide to assist students through a performance task. They are temporary learning bridges from the student to the learning. Scaffolding is very important in DI because students need varying degrees of support for the instruction to be differentiated.

Here is a guide that will help you understand stages of scaffolding: (Glatthorn, 1999, p. 115).

1. *Intensive teacher intervention:* The teacher explains exactly what is to be done. She presents a detailed model that students are to either reproduce exactly or use as a template. In teaching young children how to care for classroom animals or plants, it would make sense to have this high degree of scaffolding.

2. *Moderate teacher intervention:* The teacher makes decisions as to how much intervention the children would need to do a task. Moderate intervention could include the following. The teacher:

   ♦ Gives the students a partially completed task.
   ♦ Provides a structured prompt.
   ♦ Builds-in checkpoints for formative assessment.
   ♦ Distributes small cards containing cues, hints, suggestions.
   ♦ Does "think-alouds" for the students.
   ♦ Uses guiding questions to lead students through the task.
   ♦ Monitors flagging motivation.

3. *Limited teacher intervention:* The teacher expects a high level of independence. Bear in mind that when this happens, it shouldn't be because advanced students are given work that is below their instructional level. Students should be expected to work independently only when they are practicing or applying information and skills that were challenging for them to learn when they needed a heavier dose of teacher intervention. Limited teacher intervention can include the following:

- The teacher provides self-checking mechanisms, such as rubrics, time management plans, learning logs.
- The students provide their own scaffolding techniques.
- The students learn self-management skills.
- The teacher monitors flagging motivation.
- The teacher monitors fraying organizational skills.

References

Bartels, B. H. (1995, November–December). Promoting mathematics connections with concept mapping. *Mathematics Teaching in the Middle School.*

Benjamin, A. (2000a). *A way with words.* Auburn, MI: Teachers' Discovery.

Benjamin, A. (2000b). *An English teacher's guide to performance tasks and rubrics. Middle school and high school* (2 vols.). Larchmont, NY: Eye on Education.

Billmeyer, R. (1998). *Teaching reading in the content areas: If not me, who?* Aurora: CO: McCrel.

Bloom, H. (2000). *How to read and why.* New York: Scribner.

Caine, R. N., & Caine, G. *21st century learning initiatives.* Online.

Collins, T. (2001). *Personal paradise cards.* Carlsbad, CA: Hay House.

Dickinson, D. (1999). [Interview with Robert Sylvester, Ph.D.] *Publication.* Tucson: Zephyr Press.

Fogarty, R. (1997). *Brain compatible classrooms.* Arlington Heights, IL: Skylight.

Gardner, H. (1991). *The unschooled mind: How children think and how schools should teach.* New York: Basic Books.

Gardner, H. (1999). *Intelligence reframed.* New York: Simon & Schuster.

Gardner, H. (1983). *Frames of mind.* New York: Basic Books.

Glatthorn, A. (1999). *Performance standards and authentic learning.* Larchmont, NY: Eye on Education.

Goodman, G. (1996). *Inclusive classrooms from A to Z.* Teacher's Publishing Group.

Gregory, G., & Chapman, C. (2002). *Differentiated instructional strategies: One size doesn't fit all.* Thousand Oaks, CA: Corwin Press.

Hayakawa, S. I., & Hayakawa, A. R. (1965). *Language in thought and action.* San Diego, New York, London: Harcourt Brace.

Holloway, J. H. (1999, October). Improving the reading skills of adolescents. *Educational Leadership.* Alexandria, VA: ASCD.

Hunt, A., & Beglar, D. Dividing vocabulary into three categories. http://langue.hyper.chubu.ac.jp/jalt/pub/tlt/98/jan/hunt.html. Feb. 19, 2003.

Jensen, E. (2000). *Brain-based learning.* San Diego, CA: The Brain Store.

Kolln, M., & Funk, R. (1998). *Understanding English grammar.* Needham, MA: Allyn and Bacon.

Kotulak, B. (1996, June). Learning how to use the brain. Paper presented at the "Brain Development in Young Children: New Frontiers for Research, Policy and Practice" Conference, Chicago, on June 13, 1996.

Levine, M. (1993). *All kinds of minds.* Cambridge, MA: Educators' Publishing Service.

Longley, L. (1999, October). Gaining the arts literacy advantage. *Educational Leadership.*

Ohanian, S. (1999). *One size fits few.* Portsmouth, NH: Heinemann.

Palmer, P. J. (1997). *The courage to teach: Exploring the inner landscape of a teacher's life.* San Francisco, CA: Jossey-Bass.

Payne, R. (2002). *Understanding learning: The how, the why, the what.* Highlands, TX: aha! Process, Inc.

President's Committee on the Arts, 1999. Page 61.

Pugh, S. L., Hicks, W., Davis, M., & Venstra, T. (1992). *Bridging: A teacher's guide to metaphorical thinking.* Urbana, IL: NCTE.

Reis, S. M., & Renzulli, J. S. (2000). *Curriculum compacting: A systematic procedure for modifying the curriculum for above average ability students.* University of Connecticut: The National Research Center on the Gifted and Talented.

Thompson, M. C. (1997). *Classics in the classroom.* Royal Fireworks Press.

Thompson, M. C. (1998). *Classic words.* Royal Fireworks Press.

Tomlinson, C. A. (1999). *The differentiated classroom: Responding to the needs of all learners.* Alexandria, VA: ASCD.

Wahl, M. (1999). *Math for humans.* LivnLern Press.

Wheelock, A. (1992). *Crossing the tracks: How "untracking" can save America's schools.* New York: The New Press.

Willheim, J. (1997). *You gotta' BE the book.* New York: Columbia Teacher's College.